THE COMPLETE BOOK OF
PAINTING
TECHNIQUES
FOR THE HOME

THE COMPLETE BOOK OF
PAINTING
TECHNIQUES
FOR THE HOME

698.1

Annie Sloan & Kate Gwynn

NORTH LIGHT BOOKS

CINCINNATI, OHIO

Copyright © Collins & Brown Limited 1999

Text copyright © Annie Sloan and Kate Gwynn 1999

First published in North America
in 1998 by North Light Books
an imprint of F&W Publications, Inc.
1507 Dana Avenue
Cincinnati, OH 45207
1-800/289-0963

3 5 7 9 8 6 4 2

Library of Congress Catologing-in-Publication Data;
A catalog record for this book is available.

ISBN 0-89134-967-7

Conceived, edited and designed by Collins & Brown Limited

EDITOR: Claire Waite
DESIGNERS: Stephen Bull Associates, Paul Burcher, Sue Corner, Claire Graham
PHOTOGRAPHERS: Jon Bouchier, Geoff Dann, Michael Dunning,
Andreas Einsiedel, Shona Wood
ILLUSTRATOR: Jim Robins
PICTURE RESEARCH: Shona Wood

Reproduction by Colombia Offset (UK), London
& Hong Kong Graphics and Printing
Printed and bound by Hong Kong Graphics and Printing

Contents

Introduction

MANY YEARS AGO INTERIOR painting was only undertaken by the professional, but now, increasingly, people are trying it out for themselves and finding tremendous enjoyment. Decorative painting is rewarding, has huge possibilities, and is easy to do. People who have never considered themselves artistic find they can creatively express themselves by decorating their homes in an individual way.

An increasing interest in paint and all aspects of interior decoration is perhaps fuelled by developments in paint technology. Modern, slow-drying, water-based paint products have made a dramatic impact on the popularity of decorative paint techniques. They are easy to use, without smell, and have environmental approval. The traditional, oil-based products are becoming increasingly marginalized; there is more and more legislation against the use of oil-based paint worldwide, making the need for good-quality water-based products all the more apparent. The beauty of paint is its versatility, cheapness, practicality, and speed, and water-based products produce almost immediate results.

This book is intended for a wide range of people, from those who wish to learn and develop new decorating skills, to those already familiar with mixing colour and manipulating paint. We wanted to produce a book that is as instructive and comprehensive as possible and we have tried to make its approach accessible and clear. The techniques range from the very simple to those requiring considerable skill and knowledge. A system of stars indicates the level of difficulty of the basic techniques, so that the beginner can start on a fairly simple project and gradually build up experience and confidence. Please do not be put off if you feel that your first attempt is not wholly successful. Practice gives confidence and leads towards perfection.

The book begins with a section on colour, since an understanding of colour is vitally important to all decorative painting. Often people are motivated to paint their room with ideas taken from the natural environment; we are all familiar with the colour of rusty cans, stones, and flowers and so the colour pages with reference to these materials make a useful guide.

Each paint finish is described and illustrated on two facing pages, so that every step can be seen at a glance and followed without the need to keep turning pages backwards and forwards. Each finish has its own recipe of specific, practical advice: notes on the most suitable surfaces, the proportions for mixing oil-based glaze where necessary, a list of the materials and equipment required, and a few points which are useful to bear in mind.

Besides stencilling as a means of extra decoration, we look at making and using stamps, and freehand painting. We have used this section to bring in many elements from all over the world. As we both have training in modern art, we hope a feeling of 20th-century fine art, African and other ethnic art, and the influence of major designers, such as the Bloomsbury group, come through. There has always been a strong folk tradition of stencilling in Northern Europe, and in America and in Britain in the 19th century, decorators, such as J.D. Crace, gave stencilling a sophistication and elegance it has never lost. The freehand

ABOVE *The ceiling of the Nine Nobles' Room in Crathes Castle, Scotland is, in fact, painted on the underside of the floorboards overhead. Painted ceilings were more usual in the 16th century, particularly in Scotland. The beams were painted simply.*

painting section includes step-by-step guides for painting trompe-l'oeil effects such as playing cards on a table and stylistic skies and clouds, all of which can be done with a careful hand.

Gilding and antiquing techniques complete the decorator's repertoire. Gilding has become increasingly popular and has also broadened in style. Traditionally gilding was only used in a certain rather elegant and expensive style of decoration, but since the development of imitation metal leaf, which is easy to use, decoration has become more inventive. Copper, aluminium, and Dutch metal leaf are widely available and metallic colours can also be used in powder form. The methods of patination featured in the book, using crackleglazes, waxes, and varnishes are also integral to the vocabulary of the decorative painter.

Finally, we have included practical information and inspirational photographs of aspects of the room and various items of furniture. What to do on a ceiling for instance, some ideas for painting a cupboard, effective designs for floors, and how to paint doors and panels.

People have different approaches to paint: some handle it vigorously, others much more delicately. Consequently, one person's ragging, for example, will probably look very different from another's. Some people are classical and traditional in their approach, while others are more broadly interpretive. Whichever you are, we hope you will find these finishes and their techniques useful and easy to follow and open to individual and creative interpretation. Remember this is just the beginning. The following is taken from a book on painting and decorating;

> *Do not be ashamed of your calling.*
> *It takes five years to make a lawyer,*
> *Six a parson and seven a decorator.*

The Modern Painter and Decorator, published late 19th century.

This is not intended to put a student off, but to show how broad the subject is. The apprenticeship of a decorator in the past involved not only paint and colour mixing, but stencilling, gilding, sign-writing, principles of drawing and perspective, and general design and colour harmony. In some ways this book could be seen as a modern day apprenticeship.

Kate Gwynn   Annie Sloan

ABOVE *Old pine doors were cut down and made into shutters for a farmhouse kitchen. They were not primed and parts of the wood were saturated with turpentine. They were painted in thinned artists' oil paints and wiped with a cloth so that the colour was barely visible in parts, creating an aged and faded look. English embroidery and tapestry were used as the source for ideas. The walls were colourwashed in siennas and umbers.*

CHAPTER I

COLOUR
AND
MOOD

Don't be intimidated by colour. The limitless variations of depth and intensity created when one colour complements, absorbs, or reflects another needn't be mystifying or bewildering.

The Importance of Colour

WHEN YOU ARE STARTING off with an undecorated room, inspiration and ideas for the colour have to come from somewhere. Start with the unchangeable aspects of the room such as its use, size, orientation, and light quality. Think about when the room is used – some colours look very different in artificial light and might not be suitable for a room which is most often used in the evenings. Consider how often a room is used and think about its size. Generally, rooms which are used a great deal should be decorated in colours from the lighter side of the tonal spectrum, unless they are big enough and light enough to take a darker and richer colour. Small, frequently-used practical rooms like kitchens and bathrooms look best with light colours, unless

the room receives a lot of natural light, in which case bright and strong colours will work well. A dining room used solely for entertaining or at weekends can be made cosy and intimate by using dark, rich colours. A frequently-used home office needs to be bright and stimulating but a study used for quiet and reflection requires more muted tones.

There may be architectural features in the room that cannot be changed such as a niche or a pillar. These can either be emphasized with the application of a different colour from the rest of the room, or painted the same colour as the room to draw attention away from it.

The View

Look at the view through the windows. Are you contemplating painting green where there is already a vista of trees and fields? Perhaps the contrast of a warm brown or bright pink might be better. Take the direction in which the room faces into consideration as well. If the room faces north and has little light, warm or bright colours like yellows and pinks, are the answer. A south-facing room with lots of light is easier to decorate since most colours will work well in this situation.

Compromise

We are not all lucky enough to be decorating a blank canvas of a room, free from furniture or soft furnishings. Compromise is often inevitable as we struggle to incorporate an item like a sofa or a pair of curtains which may appear dull and dirty with the current decoration. Rather than ignoring this obstacle it is perhaps better to start here when thinking about colour choices, having also taken into consideration the size and light quality of the room. For example, if your soft furnishings encompass a patterned fabric, and the walls are going to be glazed, look at the colour of the background of the fabric. If it is beige or cream it may be a good idea to use that as your background colour rather than white.

Colours which Reflect Light

Some colours have greater luminosity than others, meaning they reflect more light. Colours like whites, creams, yellows, oranges, and bright pinks work in this way and are, therefore, good colours for small rooms. A room with light walls will seem larger because the light is reflected and bounces from one wall to another. Dark reds, greens, and blues absorb more light and make a room seem smaller. This is why they are generally recommended for larger rooms with high ceilings and plenty of natural light or for rooms where an intimate atmosphere is wanted.

Warm and Cool Colours

All colours, even browns and neutrals, can be divided into two groups, warm and cool colours. Warm colours include pinks, oranges, and reds, cool colours include blues. This difference in the temperature of colours is relative to the other colours around it. A green will appear cool if surrounded by an orange-yellow, but warm against blue-green. Generally a room needs a balance of both warm and cool colours. A room all in cool blues and greens needs a little warm brown, terracotta, or ochre. Warm-coloured walls could have a cooler colour used on the woodwork.

Tone and Colour

Tone is different from colour, and beginners sometimes find it difficult to deal with. Recognition of tonal values comes with familiarity and practice. For some it presents no problems, while others take longer to master it.

The word 'colour' refers to the hue – red, green, blue, etc. – while 'tone' refers to the lightness or darkness of the colour. Therefore a green and a blue may be the same tone, because they have the same degree of dark or light in them, even though they are different colours. Getting two or more colours to work in a room is as much to do with their tonal relationship as it is to do with their hues. A good way to see the tonal values of colours is to look at them with your eyes half closed. Colours of a similar tone will merge.

It is usual to mix all your colours, for walls and woodwork, using either a similar tone or the same colour but a few tones apart. A room in which all the colours were the same tone would be dull but a room where there is a lot of colour and a lot of tonal contrasts would be too busy and jarring on the eye. The greatest contrast in the whole range of colouring lies between black and white and these two colours certainly work well together. A third colour would have to be of equal contrast like a bright red or vivid blue. A simple rule to follow is to either use lots of colours with few tonal contrasts or lots of tonal contrasts with few colours.

Primaries, Secondaries, and Tertiaries
Red, yellow, and blue are the primary colours. They are not often used together in their pure form because they compete with each other for attention. Any two of these colours mixed together will produce what are known as the secondaries – orange (red and yellow), green (blue and yellow), and purple (red and blue). The tertiaries are colours made by mixing either two secondaries or a primary and a secondary together, making colours like khaki, tan, mustard, olive, and teal.

Complementaries
Colours also have opposites, known as complementaries. The complementary of orange is blue, that of green is red, and that of yellow is purple. Bright red and green together produce a vibrancy that the eye finds very disturbing, particularly if they are used in close proximity. If different tones of the colours are used, like rich red and dark green or pink and dark green, then the colours work very well together. Similarly, a brownish-orange and a blue can work well, whereas pure orange and pure blue have the same visually disturbing effect as red and green. In the same way, bright yellows and purples are rarely used together in decorating, but certain tones of these colours, such as creamy-yellow and lilac, complement each other very well. The walls could be painted in a muted yellow and the woodwork in a greyed lilac.

Mixing Colours
Not only can opposites be used together, they can also be mixed together to produce an interesting range of colours. If you are using an orange that is a little too bright, add a little green to darken it. By using a colour's opposite you retain colour and interest. Similarly, if you have a colour that is too simple and childlike, such as a pale blue, add a little orange for sophistication. Black, however, is a dangerous colour to mix as it kills luminosity and only makes a dirty, dull colour.

Be confident enough to mix your own colours and try not to become confused by colour clichés. For example, commercial usage has thoroughly debased peach and apricot, which now appear in a wide range from pale orange to a washed-out pink. Take your colours directly from the source of your inspiration. For instance, if you are aiming for a terracotta, bring some pots or tiles into your room to help you mix your colour.

Style in Colour
The style and atmosphere you want to create for a room – formal or informal, classic, contemporary, country – will be described as much from the colour and finish of the walls as from the furniture and other decorations. There are groups of colours which work together and bring to mind certain styles. The Victorians used nearly all tertiary colours, with a few secondaries, such as mustard, maroon, olive, and slate grey. The 1960s were distinctive for colours like cantaloupe, chocolate, lime-green, and purple. Country-style colours are mainly earth colours like ochres and siennas. Pompeian and Ancient Greek colours, successfully reworked by Robert Adam in the 18th century, are sophisticated and atmospheric. There are also Mediterranean, Scandinavian, or African colours, describing looks from other countries.

Colour Symbolism
There is an emotional response and traditional associations with certain colours, shared by people of the same culture, which can be recreated in decorating schemes. In Western culture black has been thought of as funereal, white pure, green symbolic of envy, and reds and yellows as stimulating. In other cultures white is seen as empty and related to death, green calm and good, and red as bad. Colour symbolism, which at all events from an historical point of view has an importance for decorators, has been built up on this tradition.

There is no doubt that colour is a way of expressing what we feel and affects how we feel about our surroundings. Paint not only gives protection and preservation of materials but, more importantly, it provides colour in our everyday surroundings Interesting and harmonious colours are necessary to a feeling of well being and contentment in our homes.

Blacks, Whites, and Greys

BLACK HARMONIZES WITH every colour of the spectrum. Even so, it is still a difficult colour to use, especially on large expanses. It totally absorbs light and can therefore have a depressing effect, even in the smallest area. It is often used only for pattern or detail but used as a wall colour together with lots of colour and pattern it can look stunning and dramatic. It should rarely be used to darken other colours, as it has a tendency to kill them.

There is more than one black of course. Black can be a very dark tint of virtually any colour. A very dark green for instance can be more interesting than a plain black, as can blue-black or brown-black. A selection of more subtle and interesting variations can be produced by mixing black with blue, deep red, or brown, for example. Black is not generally used as a base colour since the idea of glazing is to give colours depth by reflecting light. If black is used to colour a glaze for techniques such as ragging or colourwashing, it will appear grey, especially if it is used over a white base. If used over colours the effect can be strong, especially when the colour is condensed as it is with combing, sponging and, to a certain extent, dragging. If used over a yellow base the result can look quite green.

Whites

White, of course, harmonizes with every colour. As the opposite of black, it reflects light and can look bright and optimistic. It can provide a wonderful foil for other colours or be used as the main colour, with neutrals to complement it. It can be sophisticated or it can be empty and stark. There are an enormous number of different whites. In India, they say

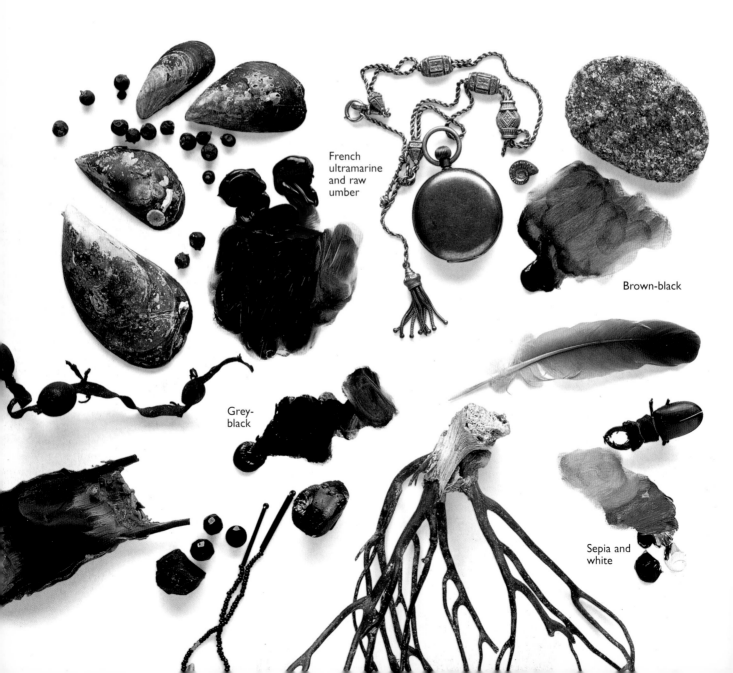

French ultramarine and raw umber

Brown-black

Grey-black

Sepia and white

there are four tones of white – the green-white of the sea, the blue-white of the clouds, the yellow-white of the moon, and the pink-white of the conch shell. Added to that might be the slightly browned or greyed whites of linen, damask, lace, canvas, and ecru.

A white glaze is unusual but quite possible and could be used over almost any colour either light, bright, or dark. A white glaze will produce a misty look when used in an all over effect like ragging or colourwashing and will be more defined if dragging or combing is used. When working with white you may find that you need to use a lot of paint to colour the glaze.

Greys

Greys tend to be rather ambiguous and difficult-to-classify colours, mainly because they vary so greatly in both temperature and character.

Rather like a chameleon, grey takes on the colour of its surroundings and is often used as a neutral. Grey can absorb light or reflect it depending on whether it is near black like slate-grey or a very light, near-white grey. The obvious way to mix a grey is by adding white to black, but this produces a cold, lifeless colour with little character. It is better to use a variety of colours with white to give more dimensional greys. Mixing blues with umbers and white makes a cool grey, and combining pinks with greens and white will result in a warmer shade. A mix of two complementaries with white will produce interesting shades, for example orange and some blue combined with white makes a warm grey and yellow with purple and white makes a taupe colour. If the colour you have mixed is too cool, add red to it to bring warmth.

As a base colour, grey can have a rather deadening effect on a coloured glaze, although some marbles, like Saint Remi, stipulate a brown-grey base. Grey glazes can be used over black, white, or muted or pale bases such as pink. If using oil-based glaze do not use Payne's grey unless used thickly, the yellow in the glaze will turn the blue in the paint to green.

French ultramarine, burnt umber, and white

Alizarin crimson, green-blue, blue-grey, and white

White and raw sienna

White

White and brown-black

15

Off-whites

OFF-WHITES ARE tints of white with a hint of another colour added. They can be bland but, at their best, they are mellow and sophisticated. Off-whites are extremely useful as neutral decorators' colours, and help to blend and harmonize the entire spectrum. Examples of off-whites include biscuit, fawn, honey, beige, and stone.

Off-whites reflect light, but they are not bright like pure white. They often take on the colours around them and their appearance varies in different contexts.

Some of the off-whites are warm colours with a yellow or pink tint. For a cool off-white, raw umber with white produces a greyish-mushroom colour. Blue or green with one of the umbers and white will also give a cool off-white.

Off-whites are often used as a base coat for muted glaze colours, to encourage the mellow feel of the colours in the glaze. A frequently-used and classic combination, particularly for dragging on woodwork, is a raw umber and white glaze over a white or off-white base.

White, warm brown, and raw umber

White and raw umber

White and burnt umber

White, raw sienna, and raw umber

Yellows

YELLOW IS A WARM colour which radiates light and a sunny exuberance, and so is a good colour to use in a room that is naturally dark . There is really no such thing as a dark yellow: as it becomes dark it ceases to be a yellow but becomes brown.

The range of yellows is very small, there are the greenish, sharp yellows, the coolest of the yellows, the mid- and orange-tinged egg-yolk yellows (cadmium and chrome yellow), and the earth yellows (yellow ochre and raw sienna). There are also pale yellows, where white has been added to create a cream or ivory shade. Despite this small range, yellow has several different characteristics. There are the slightly aloof lemon-yellows, the mellow earth yellows, and the young, sunny mid-yellows.

Most yellows in the decorator's palette tend towards the mustard and egg-yolk colours rather than the greenish tinge of lemon. This is probably because of the difficult nature of yellow, which changes with artificial light. Pale yellows simply disappear at night, drowned out by the yellow night lights, while a bright lemon-yellow (with green in it) may just look very acid, with the green taking prominence. Therefore it is particularly important with this colour to do a test patch, to check the effect at night.

In glazes, the earth-coloured yellows are favoured since they have the strength to keep their colour when diluted in glaze, and are surprisingly bright. To vary a mid-yellow glaze add browns, or oranges, with or without white. The complementary of yellow is purple so this can be added to deepen and darken yellows. A good base for a yellow glaze, apart from white, is pale orange, which will give a warm overall effect. If a really intense colour is wanted then the base colour must be a pale yellow with a strong yellow glaze over it.

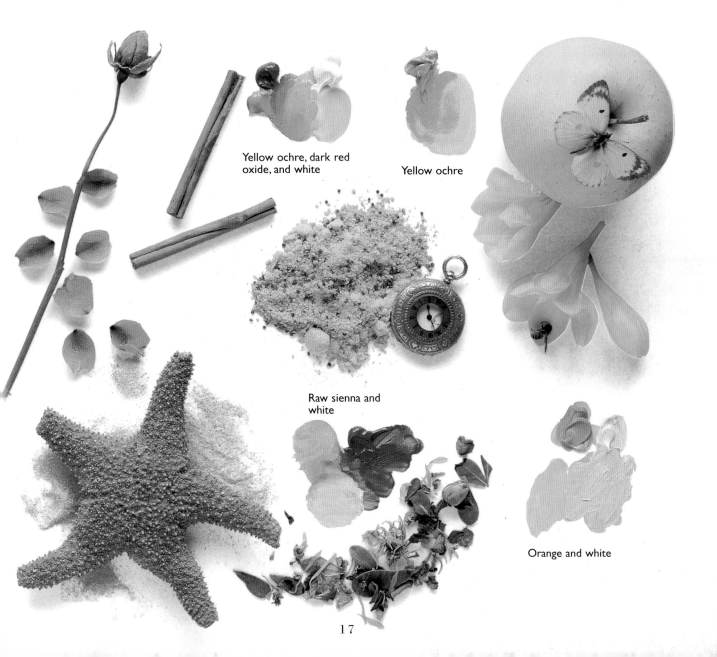

Yellow ochre, dark red oxide, and white

Yellow ochre

Raw sienna and white

Orange and white

17

Blues

THERE IS A RICH and varied choice of blues and they encompass probably the widest range of contrasts of all the colours in the spectrum. Blues can be pale and near white in shade – chalky and baby blue – or dark and near black – navy and military blue.

In hue, the range covers exotic green-tinged blues – peacock, turquoise, and tropical sea-blue – through the clean mid-blues – cornflower, china-blue, and lapis lazuli – to the purplish varieties of lilac, heliotrope, and lavender.

Blue can be very clear and simple – a summer's sky, sea, and traditional gingham – but with the addition of brown or orange a more mysterious and complex range.of blue-greys can be made, resulting in both warm and cool shades like Wedgwood, duck-egg, and Swedish blue.

The blue pigments range from green-blue (Prussian blue) to reddish-blue (ultramarine) with a strong mid-blue (cobalt). All the other blues are made from these, usually with the addition of white, lemon-yellow, copper, green, umbers, or sienna.

Green-blue, blue-green, and white

Burnt umber, blue-green, and white

French ultramarine and white

Cobalt and white

In the past the use of blue in oil-based glazes was quite a difficult process since the linseed oil in the glaze caused a yellowing effect and the blue inevitably became quite green. Large quantities of white had to be added to counteract the yellowing. As white is a very opaque colour this gave the glaze less translucency and therefore less depth. Because of this many people avoided blue altogether, perhaps fuelling the idea that blue is a difficult colour to use in decoration.

Nowadays water-based glazes are used which are non-yellowing, so eliminating the problem. Of course there are still blues that are cool and not conducive to a cosy atmosphere, making them difficult to work with, but there are also many warm, comforting blues which are a pleasure to live with. It is best to avoid grey- or green-blues, brown- or purple-blues,

and very dark blues, which can look cool and uninviting both by association and by the way that blue tends to absorb light. Look for blues with a lot of red content, like ultramarine, which are warming shades.

To achieve successful results the base colour used with blue glazes is very important. A yellow base will give a mid-blue glaze a turquoise look, but a purple-blue glaze over a yellow base is more likely to result in an unattractive grey. To make the blue strong and vibrant, a harsh, bright electric blue should be used for the base with a strong, fairly deep blue in the glaze. For a blue like a summer sky with lots of depth and brightness a white or pale blue base could be used with a cobalt mid-blue glaze. A pink base will give a warm glow to an ultramarine glaze.

French ultramarine,
burnt umber, and
white

French ultramarine,
alizarin crimson, and
white

Reds

THERE ARE RELATIVELY few reds which we can really call red, compared to the huge range of blues and greens. Reds are the groups of colours between purple and orange. Reds that are a little purple and have no yellow in them are the deep crimson colours which absorb light but give warmth, like burgundy, mahogany, and ox blood. When reds are nearer the orange end of the spectrum they are bright, glowing, and reflective like the reds of tomatoes, strawberries, and geraniums. A real red has no white in it. As soon as white is added it becomes pink.

The two groups of red mineral pigments are the bright cadmium and vermilion pigments and the darker, crimson shades of alizarin. The earth pigments called Indian red and light red are, in fact, brown.

Mixing a true red is difficult to do when using oil-based glazes, which cause the bright mineral pigments to fade. With water-based glazes, however, this is no longer a problem and a vibrant tomato-red glaze can be easily made.

A base colour needs to project light or be pale, so red is rarely used in this role. Oranges or pinks, pale or bright, are generally used as the base for a red glaze. The end result will be deeper if you use a strong base colour, for instance strong pink is a good base colour for a crimson effect. A red glaze over a white base will look pinkish and lack strength.

Alizarin crimson and dark green

Alizarin crimson and white

Alizarin crimson and yellow ochre

Alizarin crimson and warm brown

Alizarin crimson and French ultramarine

Greens

THE RANGE OF GREENS – from yellowish lime-greens through to bluish turquoise-greens – is very wide and covers many characteristics. There are muted, acid, bright, intense, pale, and deep greens. Greens fall between blue and red in the colour spectrum and so, generally, they are neither hot nor cold. The exceptions, however, are the blue-tinged shades of the turquoises or aquamarines, which, because of their high blue content, can be very cold. The lighter and brighter greens, particularly the yellow-greens, project light more than the deeper, muted, or blue-greens.

Amongst the earth pigments you will find the muted green of terre-vert and chromium of oxide, whilst green mineral pigments include the bluish, copper colours of phthalocyanine, often called viridian.

The usual way to mix green is to combine blue with yellow. This, however, can be difficult and can easily result in a dull, crude green. Instead, greens can be mixed in quite a number of ways. There are some surprising mixtures, such as lemon-yellow combined with black to make olive. It is best to mix with a lemon-yellow rather than an egg-yolk yellow; the red in the egg-yolk yellow will not mix well with blue, resulting in a disappointing, muddy colour.

All the greens work well in a glaze and with all the different finishes. Depending on the depth of colour wanted the base colour can be white, yellow, blue, or green, either pale or bright. A yellow-coloured base used under a mid- or yellow-green glaze makes a fresh, grass-green. To make a rich, intense green use a mid-green glaze over a bright green base.

Dark green, yellow ochre, and white

Dark green and primrose

Green-blue and white

Green-blue and raw umber

Pinks

PINK IS BASICALLY a red with white added, but the character of pink is very different from that of red. A rich variety of pinks can be mixed from the basic red and white, and whether these are bright and intense or pale, the colour will always be warm.

There are two very distinctive types of pink which can be mixed. One type is the clean pinks made from crimson and true red pigments such as cadmium, vermilion, and alizarin. The other group are the, brownish-pinks made from earth pigments like Indian and Venetian red.

The first group make very simple pinks. Using crimson mixed with white a magenta-tinged pink can be made. This basic pink can be adjusted with the addition of more white or more red to become either bright, shocking, or raspberry-

pink. From mid-reds and white come strawberry-pinks and the colour of prawns and salmon. When these pinks are strong they are vivid and lively but when they are pale they can become the sickly-sweet colours that people normally associate with baby pink.

The brownish, earth reds combined with white make a complex pink, like the pale, terracotta-pink seen on limewashed houses in the Mediterranean, North Africa, and India. These dirty, washed-out pinks work particularly well in decorating.

White, pale pink, orange, and yellow all make good base colours for an earthy pink glaze. A bright pink can be used as the base for a red or orange glaze to make a very strong, intense and glowing colour. Pinks also mix well with rather sombre tones of green and blue.

Red oxide
and white

Dark red oxide
and white

Pale red oxide,
yellow ochre,
and white

Pale red oxide
and white

Alizarin
crimson, white,
and dark green

Browns

BROWN COLOURS RANGE from deep orange-terracottas and rich chocolate to lighter pinky-browns and beige colours. Browns can be both warm and cool, and as dark or as pale as you like.

The brown colours generally stem from two groups of earth pigments – oxides and umbers. The oxides, sometimes called red ochres, are warm rust and terracotta coloured and can be found all over the world. Some, like Indian red, contain a hint of purple caused by the presence of manganese, while others, like burnt sienna, are verging on orange. They will become pinky-brown when white is added. These browns are useful for interior decorating because they are warm and work well with a lot of other colours, particularly blues and greens.

Burnt umber is a warm, chocolate-brown earth pigment and raw umber is a cool, greenish-brown. The umbers have a less obvious impact than the oxides, but they make subtle decorating colours. They have been popularly used with white to make a sophisticated range of pale browns and putty colours.

Terracotta-browns can be rich and opulent when used over a bright base colour like sharp orange or shocking pink. When they are used sparingly in a glaze over a pale or white base colour, the result will be light orange or pink.

The umber-browns have traditionally been used over white or off-white, in particular when dragging on woodwork.

For woodgraining it is essential to mix a good range of browns, from light oaks through to walnut and mahogany.

Burnt umber and white

Dark red oxide and white

Dark red oxide

Dark red oxide, yellow ochre, and white

Warm brown and white

CHAPTER II

MATERIALS
AND
EQUIPMENT

You can decorate with a single brush and some paint, but a look at the range of extra materials and specialist tools may inspire you to be that bit more adventurous.

Preparing Surfaces

FULL OF ENTHUSIASM and buoyed-up with ideas it is all too easy to start decorating without preparing properly. Painting a room in an exciting new finish can be very quick indeed, but it still requires a certain amount of planning and organization beforehand.

Remove everything from the walls and put all the furniture in the middle of the room, or take it out of the room so that you have good access to the walls and they can be viewed from a distance. Sweep or vacuum the surfaces to be decorated, as moving furniture is bound to cause dust to fly in the air. Traditionally decorators use a short-handled brush like a robust, thick-bristled paintbrush to sweep the surfaces.

Dustsheets should be placed everywhere, particularly over carpets. Painters' dustsheets are the best for protection. While old sheets and curtains are helpful, nothing quite beats the traditional cloth, which is large and very absorbent. If you have fitted carpets place masking tape along the walls so that the skirting-board/baseboard can be painted easily. There are several different types of masking tape, each with their own particular character. One is able to stretch and curve around awkward shapes and corners but is very sticky. Others have a low tack and cannot be bent or curved.

Cracks in walls will need filling, while furniture which is to be decorated should be stripped of old paint or varnish and cleared of wax.

Paint your base coat with a roller or brush depending on what is easiest for you. If you are using a very large pot of paint, decant some into a more manageable-sized can or a roller tray. If you are using a brush at corners and edges you may find it useful to carry a can with a handle. Have water and a sponge at hand to mop up any accidental spills. Finally, give yourself plenty of time to do the job properly.

Dusting brush
A robust brush can be used to dust clean the surface to be decorated, particularly at the edges and corners.

Filler
Fill cracks or holes in walls by applying a commercial filler using a trowel.

Paint stripper
Commercial paint and varnish remover should be applied with an old bristle brush.

Protective gloves
Protective gloves can be worn during all the preparation techniques, but it is essential that they are worn when using paint stripper.

Sandpaper
Different grades of sandpaper are available, from coarse to very fine, including wet-and-dry sandpaper for a really smooth surface.

Wax remover
To clear a surface of old wax you will need to use a specialized wax remover which is applied with steel wool.

Masking tape
Decorator's masking tape is available in different thicknesses and different levels of tackiness. Use it at the skirting-board/baseboard to protect fitted carpets from paint.

Roller and paint tray
A roller is a good tool for applying paint over large surfaces.

Dustsheet
Painters' dustsheets are absorbent and large and should be used to protect furniture and carpets from paint spills. It is also useful to have plenty of cloth on hand for cleaning away mistakes.

Household paintbrushes
Household paintbrushes of different sizes can be used to apply the base coat. They are also useful for applying a glaze coat.

Paint can
Decant your paint into a manageable-sized container. One with a handle is very useful.

Brushes

USING THE RIGHT BRUSH for the job makes an enormous difference. Struggling with a brush that is the wrong shape or size can leave you feeling tired and despondent. Having said that, it would be a mistake to spend money on brushes unnecessarily, before you have grasped the fundamentals of your chosen decorative technique.

The brushes you will need are available from good decorating and paint shops, or from specialist artists' suppliers. The specialist brushes on these pages represent just part of the choice available. There are an enormous number of artists' fitches, for example, in a variety of sizes and shapes. Most decorative painters will use several, each with different characteristics suitable for different jobs. Some fitches, the longer-bristled, round-ended brushes for instance, can be used for many different decorative techniques and so are invaluable. Other brushes have much more limited use but are invaluable for certain specific jobs.

Many student-quality brushes are reasonably priced and will let you learn and carry out the basic technique without breaking the bank. Later, if you are doing a lot of decorative painting, or even become professional, higher-quality brushes are a good investment: they will last a long time and produce excellent, consistent results.

On a good-quality brush the paint flows well and with ease. The cheaper-quality brush has bristles which are stiff, with less spring, and the bristles are not as well packed as they are on a more expensive brush. An old, worn-down brush can be used as you practise a new technique.

In order to keep your brushes for as long as possible, especially the more expensive ones, careful washing is essential. Brushes used with water-based products should be cleaned with water and liquid detergent as soon as possible after use, before the plastics in the products dry. If water-based products dry on the brush then soak them in methylated spirits, which may loosen the plastic. Oil-based products on brushes need to be thinned using white spirit/mineral spirits or turpentine, before rinsing in warm water. Generally, people are not generous enough with the thinner.

Stippling brushes
A stiff-bristle brush for lifting off fine dots of glaze. These are available in many different sizes and in student and professional quality. Student-quality brushes are good for use with water-based products.

Dragging brush
A long, coarse-bristled brush used for dragging, and some woodgraining.

Flogging brush
Flogging brushes have longer bristles than dragging brushes and are used for dragging, flogging, moiré, and oak graining.

Woodgraining brush
This specialist brush can be used to make the initial grained effect.

Bristle pencil overgrainer
Used for woodgraining with oil-based products.

Sable pencil overgrainer
Used for woodgraining with water-based products.

Short-bristled flat brushes
These brushes can be used in many different ways and for many different techniques, including colourwashing, dragging, and varnishing large areas.

Badger-hair softening brush
Used to blend and soften many effects, especially faux finishes, and give a smooth surface. Badger hair is very soft and flexible.

Hog-hair softening brush
Used to blend and soften some paint finishes. Hog hair produces a firm but flexible, quality brush.

Badger-hair softening brushes
These student-quality brushes are a cheaper alternative to the expensive, professional-quality softening brushes.

Swordliner and fine artist's brush
Use a swordliner to make veins in marble. Artists' brushes, for lining and details, are available with different hair and bristle mixes.

Fitches
Fitches are long-handled brushes available with rounded or flat ferrules, rounded, squared, chiselled, or pointed bristle ends, and with long or short bristles.

Sponges, Rags, and Combs

VARIOUS MATERIALS are used to manipulate a glaze and create decorative paint finishes. For some techniques specialist brushes are needed, while in other cases sponges, rags, or combs create the decorative effect.

Sponges can be used to both apply and remove glaze, either on their own or as part of another technique, such as marbling. Originally only natural marine sponges were available, but you can now buy sponges cut with irregular holes which imitate the pattern that a natural sponge makes. Their angular shape will affect the overall result, and should be taken into consideration. Thin kitchen sponges should not be used to create a paint finish but they are useful for cleaning and wiping away mistakes.

A large amount of cotton rag is needed to rag or rag roll walls and furniture. Old cotton sheets are good to use, because they are soft and make a fine and delicate effect. You can use other types of cloth but avoid those with a high nylon or polyester content, which are not absorbent.

Mutton cloth, also called stockinet, is a stretchy, knitted material, which gives glaze an uneven texture. It is used on its own and is also useful for lifting off surplus glaze and softening the effect of many faux finishes. Always buy cotton mutton cloth, not the nylon variety.

It is interesting to experiment with all types of fabric, but remember that you will use a substantial amount and should always have sufficient at hand to finish the project.

Combs originated from woodgraining techniques, but are now also used on their own. These are usually manufactured from rubber but home-made combs can be cut out of plastic floor tiles or cardboard. Specialist woodgraining tools can be bought at most good paint shops and have different attachments to imitate different types of wood.

Synthetic sponge
A thick sponge with holes cut into it can be used in the same way as a natural sponge.

Natural marine sponge
Each natural sponge is different and will produce a different effect in the glaze.

Rag
Old cotton sheets and old, mainly cotton clothes can be used in decorative paint techniques.

Flat, kitchen sponge
This sponge should only be used for cleaning. It is not suitable as a paint effect tool.

Graduated comb
This soft, rubbery comb has teeth of graduating widths.

Graining rollers
Graining rollers are used to imitate the grain of certain woods. They are pulled through the glaze and rocked at the same time. These rubber rollers are particularly good for use with water-based products and come in different sizes.

Triangular comb
Each side of the comb has differently-spaced teeth.

Heartgrainer
The plastic, removable head can be changed to produce a wide, oak grain or a fine, pine grain. Plastic tools are particularly good for use with oil-based products, although they can be used with water-based materials.

Home-made combs
You can make your own combs by cutting plastic floor tiles or cardboard with a sharp, heavy-duty knife.

Mutton cloth
Used in many faux finishes as well as for simple mutton clothing.

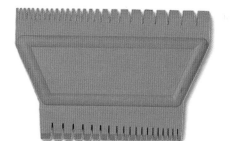

Paints and Glazes

To produce a wide range of paint finishes from ragging and sponging to marbling and woodgraining, three ingredients are needed. The base paint, the glaze, and the colouring medium for the glaze.

Paint finishes can be completed using oil- or water-based systems. For many, water-based products are the simplest solution. They are easy to colour and use, they dry quickly and without smell, and brushes can be washed in water after use. Many professionals prefer to use oil-based products however, since their slower drying time makes large walls easier to manage. Also, advanced techniques like marbling are given greater depth with the use of oil-based products.

The coloured glaze is best applied on a base coat which is non-absorbent. This means using a mid-sheen, water-based paint like vinyl silk/satin latex. A glossy, oil-based surface will reject the water-based glaze and a matt surface will absorb it. A mid-sheen oil-based paint such as oil eggshell should be used as the base for oil-based glazes.

Glaze is a colourless, slow-drying, transparent medium to which pigment or paint is added. Coloured glaze is applied over the base coat and manipulated with a tool such as a brush or rag to reveal, in places, the base colour underneath.

Traditionally, oil-based glazes were used for decorative painting, but in recent years there have been tremendous developments in water-based glazes and these have become very popular. There are also precoloured glazes available.

The most common method of colouring water-based glazes is to add some water-based paint. The more paint added the darker the colour will be but the quicker the glaze will dry. Powder pigments can be used to colour glaze on their own, or they can be added to the paint and glaze system. To colour oil-based glazes use artists' oil paints or powder pigments.

Low-vinyl decorative paints have little plastic content and are available from specialist paint shops. They are ideal for painting furniture, stencilling, and antiquing techniques, and are also good for colouring water-based glazes.

Oil-based glaze
The linseed oil in this traditional glaze medium has a yellowing effect. Oil-based glaze has a flashpoint of 40C/104F so glaze-soaked rags should be spread out to dry before being thrown away.

Water-based glaze
An easy-to-use modern medium, water-based glazes look white in the container but when brushed out are completely colourless and transparent.

Thinner
Oil-based glaze needs either white spirit/mineral spirits or turpentine added to it to thin the paint and glaze mixture.

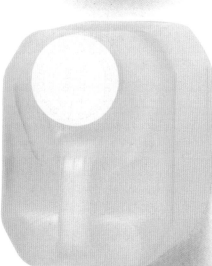

Precoloured glazes
Glazes can also be bought already coloured. Some, like this one, are stained warm brown for woodgraining and others are stained in pale tints.

Powder pigments
These are pure pigments in powder form. When you use them to colour glaze you must make sure they have absorbed completely and will not produce spots of uneven colour.

Artists' oil paints
These can only be mixed into oil-based glaze, and need to be diluted first with a little thinner, to allow for ease of mixing. They also need to be thinned if they are to be used on their own.

Water-based paint
Use water-based paint to colour water-based glaze. A low-vinyl decorative paint or matt emulsion/flat latex paint can be used. Remember that the colour will be somewhat diluted in strength in the glaze. Low-vinyl paints can also be used for stencilling and freehand painting.

Base paint
Mid-sheen paints (satin or eggshell) should be used as the base coat for glaze to be applied over. As a general rule, use a water-based base coat when using water-based glaze and an oil-based base coat when using oil-based glaze. A dark glaze will look good over a light base coat and a light glaze will benefit from a dark base colour.

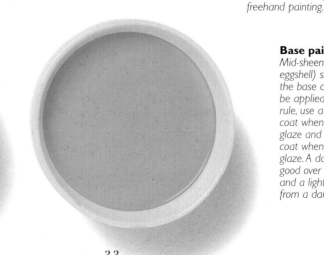

Stencilling and Stamping

THE ESSENTIAL IDEA of stencilling has remained the same for centuries, but in recent years the materials have changed and developed, much for the better. Once you have found the design you want to recreate, you now have a choice of methods for doing so.

You can transfer your design using tracing paper to a sheet of stencil card, and cut out the motif using a craft knife over a board or a special self-healing cutting mat. Although expensive, these cutting mats are very useful since, unlike wooden board that quickly becomes ridged with score marks, these mats are not affected by sharp knife cuts and do not interfere with subsequent cutting.

Alternatively you can cut your design from acetate, a transparent material which you can trace your motif on to directly. To cut acetate you can use a craft knife or a special heat knife over a sheet of glass. The heat knife involves less effort than

the craft knife as little hand pressure needs to be applied. Using acetate and a heat knife gives a cleaner result, with a smoother line than can be achieved with stencil card.

There are also, of course, many ready-cut stencils available, made from a variety of papers and plastic sheets.

In addition to traditional stencil brushes, which are designed to hold small amounts of paint, stencil designs can also be applied using foam rollers or natural and synthetic sponges (see pp. 30–31). Dabbing with a sponge is quicker than using stencil brushes. Spray paint can also be used.

Stamping is a relatively new technique borrowed from past traditions of fabric and wallpaper printing. You can use a sharp knife to cut your own stamps from a variety of materials such as sponge, polystyrene packaging material, or potatoes and other vegetables. There are also many ready-made printing blocks available.

Cutting mat
A self-healing cutting mat is a worthwhile investment if you plan to make many stencils yourself.

Sheet of glass
When cutting acetate with a heat knife work over a sheet of glass.

Acetate
An acetate stencil is easy to cut and use. The transparent material makes it easy to position repeat designs.

Stencil card and ready-printed stencils
Stencil card is sturdy and can be handled many times. These ready-designed stencils (far left) come ready to cut.

Pencil
When making a repeat pattern it is a good idea to mark a grid on your surface to record the repeats.

Stencil brushes
Stencil brushes come in many different shapes and sizes. They are usually stiff-bristled.

Roller and tray
Small rollers like this are perfect for stencilling, and can also be used to apply paint to a stamp.

Heat knife
An electronic heat knife is the quickest and easiest tool to use when cutting acetate.

Ready-made stamp
Ready-made stamps are available in a wide range of motifs.

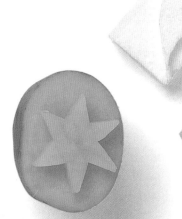

Craft knife
A sharp craft knife should be used to cut a design into stencil card and can also be used to cut acetate.

Home-made stamps
You can make your own stamps by cutting into polystyrene, sponge, or vegetables. You do not always have to cut a motif, sometimes a simple shape like the sponge diamond will produce a lot of textural interest.

Gilding and Antiquing

YOU MAY WISH to embellish a decorated surface further by adding a metallic finish or giving it an aged effect. Traditional gilding is an ancient art which can be mastered with practice, but developments in gilding materials mean there is now an easier technique to follow. The materials used for antiquing surfaces are also much developed.

Traditional gilding uses some very particular tools. Gilders use real gold in largely loose-leaf form, cut and prepared on a gilder's pad and applied to a gessoed surface using a gilder's tip, before being burnished to a high shine. Decorative gilders today, however, can make use of modern materials, such as transfer metal leaf and commercial gold size, which make the technique quicker and easier to carry out.

The effects of age can be imitated using a number of methods. Varnish or wax can be coloured or distressed while commercial products can be used to cause cracks to appear on the surface. Traditional methods of causing a crackled effect relied on the incompatibility of oil and water but developments in acrylics mean there are now products available that use solely water-based materials.

Brushes
The gilder's mop (below) gently presses the leaf on to the surface without tearing it. Use a bristle brush (right) to apply gesso.

Bronze powders
Bronze powders (left) can be applied to a surface on their own or mixed with clear or neutral wax.

Gesso
Mix whiting (top) and rabbit-skin glue (bottom) to make gesso, or buy it ready-made.

Gold size
Oil-based (top) and water-based (bottom) sizes are specialized glues used to adhere metal leaf and bronze powders.

Traditional gilding
Real gold leaf is prepared on a gilder's pad which protects the delicate leaf. The gilder's tip is used to pick up the thin leaf.

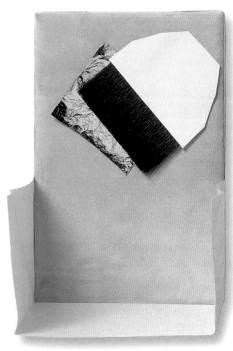

Metal leaf
Metal leaf comes in loose (far left) and transfer (below) forms. The transfer leaf is easier to handle.

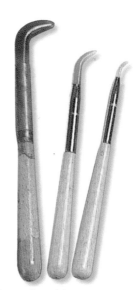

Agate burnishers
Smooth burnishers prevent the gold leaf from being torn.

Gilder's knife
This knife is not very sharp and is used to cut delicate gold leaf.

Varnishes
Oil- (left) or water-based (right) varnishes can be used in antiquing techniques. They can be coloured with pigment and distressed with steel wool.

Varnish brushes
Flat-ended varnish brushes should be used for antiquing effects.

Artists' oil paint
Artists' oil paints are used to accentuate the cracks formed by crackle varnish.

Powder pigments
Use powder pigments to age a surface by brushing it into varnish while it is still wet.

Coarse steel wool
Use coarse steel wool to scratch a varnished surface, making it appear old and worn.

Crackle varnish
This two-part system consists of a base varnish (left) and a crackle varnish (right). The crackle varnish reacts with the base varnish and cracks are formed on drying.

Crackleglaze
The water-based crackleglaze medium is applied between two coats of water-based paint. The top coat reacts with the crackleglaze and cracks develop in the paint.

Dark wax
Use fine steel wool to apply a dark wax before scratching it back with coarse steel wool to imitate the effects of wear and tear.

Varnishing and Waxing

To PROTECT YOUR WORK and to obtain a particular look or feel, a surface can be given a coat of varnish or wax. Although often hurriedly done, finishing is an important part of the decorating process if you want your work to last.

To get the very best in protection, a varnish is needed; it requires little upkeep and can come into contact with hot or wet things without fear of spoiling. The traditional oil-based varnish is strong and dries with a yellowish tinge which can give your work depth. However, oil-based varnish is slow-drying, which means that dust particles can easily drop on to it before it dries. Water-based acrylic varnishes are very popular because they are quick-drying, odourless, and colourless. Both types are available in matt, mid-sheen/satin, and gloss finishes, although only water-based varnishes are truly dead flat.

Varnish can be applied with any brush, in theory, but the job will be much more efficient and pleasing if completed using a proper varnish brush. A flat-ended brush with quite long bristles and a certain amount of flexibility is ideal. Acrylic fibres are effective with water-based varnishes while natural fibres work best with oil-based varnishes.

Waxes also protect your work, though not as well as varnishes. They produce a soft, mellow finish which can be buffed to a silky sheen.

Waxes are best applied to an absorbent surface with a fine steel wool. The steel wool allows the solvents in the wax to penetrate the surface you are working on.

Powder pigments can be added to varnish or wax to give an extra dimension to the finish.

Acrylic-fibre varnish brushes
These specialist varnish brushes, in varying sizes, are ideal for work with water-based varnishes.

Natural-fibre varnish brush
This varnish brush, with natural-fibre bristles, should be used to apply oil-based varnish.

Oil-based varnish
Oil-based varnish, sometimes called polyurethane varnish, dries with a slight yellow tinge.

Water-based varnish
Water-based varnish, also known as acrylic varnish, dries completely clear.

Cotton cloth
A cotton cloth is used to buff a waxed surface to a soft sheen.

Dark wax
A dark-coloured wax will give your surface an aged or antiqued look.

Clear wax
Clear wax imparts a soft, attractive sheen to the surface. Neutral wax, which is off-white in appearance, has the same effect.

Powder pigments
You can add pigment to wet varnish on a surface or mix it in with some wax for a coloured finish.

Fine steel wool
Use the finest grade of steel wool to apply wax.

Suitability of Surfaces

	NEW PLASTER	OLD UNEVEN WALLS	WALLPAPER	RAISED/ WOODCHIP PAPER	HESSIAN	STONE-WORK/ BRICKWORK
Preparing to paint (see pp. 42–43)	Leave to dry out for six months.	Fill holes or cracks.	Apply two coats of paint before working.	Apply two coats of paint before working.	Apply several coats of paint. It will retain its texture.	Apply several coats of paint. It will retain its texture.
Mutton clothing (see pp. 48–49)	Good	Good	Good	Possible	Impossible	Possible
Ragging (see pp. 50–51)	Good	Good	Good	Possible	Possible	Possible
Frottage (see pp. 52–53)	Good	Good	Good	Good	Possible	Good
Stippling (see pp.54–55)	Good	Possible	Good	Possible	Impossible	Possible
Rag rolling (pp. 56–57)	Good	Possible	Good	Possible	Impossible	Possible
Sponging on/sponging off (see pp. 58–61)	Good	Good	Good	Good	Possible	Good
Colourwashing (see pp. 62–63)	Good	Good	Good	Good	Good	Good
Dragging (see pp.64–66)	Good	Possible	Good	Possible	Impossible	Good
Flogging (see p. 67)	Good	Possible	Good	Possible	Impossible	Possible
Combing (see pp. 68–69)	Good	Possible	Good	Impossible	Impossible	Impossible
Spattering (see pp. 70–71)	Good	Good	Good	Possible	Possible	Possible
Sienna marble/ Breccia marble (see pp. 76–83 and 86–87)	Good	Possible	Good	Impossible	Impossible	Impossible
Floating marble (see pp. 84–85)	Impossible	Impossible	Impossible	Impossible	Impossible	Impossible
Malachite/porphyry/ lapis lazuli/agate (see pp. 90–98) *Not usually done in large areas.*	Good	Possible	Good	Impossible	Impossible	Impossible
Granite (see p. 99)	Good	Possible	Good	Possible	Possible	Possible
Tortoiseshell (see pp. 100–101) *Not usually done in large areas.*	Good	Impossible	Good	Impossible	Impossible	Impossible
Moiré (see pp. 102–103)	Good	Possible	Good	Impossible	Impossible	Impossible
Woodgraining (see pp. 104–111)	Good	Possible	Good	Impossible	Impossible	Impossible
Stencilling and stamping (see pp. 114–125)	Good	Good	Good	Possible	Possible	Possible
Gilding (see pp. 138–145)	Good	Possible	Good	Possible	Inappropriate	Possible
Crackle varnish (see pp. 146–147) *Large surfaces are difficult to tackle.*	Good	Possible	Possible	Impossible	Impossible	Impossible
Crackleglaze (see pp. 148–149) *Large surfaces are difficult to tackle.*	Good	Good	Good	Good	Possible	Possible

FINE CORK TILING	CONCRETE FLOOR	FLOOR-BOARDS	WOOD-WORK	FURNITURE	CARVED SURFACES	GLASS	METAL	LAMINATE/SHINY SURFACE
Seal with paint or sealer.	Apply water-based paint. Varnish with floor varnish.	Clean thoroughly. Remove stains and varnishes. Varnish with floor varnish.	Gloss paint must be stripped or rubbed with steel wool or sandpaper.	Remove old varnish and paint. Rub down.	Remove old varnish and paint. Rub down.	Clean thoroughly.	Remove rust. Apply metal paint or water-based paint.	Clean thoroughly. Use water-based paints, low-vinyl is best.
Good	Inappropriate	Inappropriate	Possible	Good	Good	Inappropriate	Possible	Possible
Good	Inappropriate	Inappropriate	Possible	Good	Possible	Inappropriate	Possible	Possible
Good	Possible	Possible	Possible	Good	Possible	Inappropriate	Possible	Possible
Good	Inappropriate	Inappropriate	Possible	Possible	Good	Inappropriate	Possible	Possible
Good	Inappropriate	Inappropriate	Possible	Good	Possible	Inappropriate	Possible	Possible
Good	Possible	Possible	Possible	Good	Good	Inappropriate	Possible	Possible
Good	Possible	Possible	Possible	Good	Good	Possible	Possible	Possible
Good	Inappropriate	Inappropriate	Good	Good	Impossible	Inappropriate	Possible	Possible
Good	Inappropriate	Inappropriate	Good	Good	Impossible	Inappropriate	Possible	Possible
Good	Possible	Possible	Good	Good	Impossible	Inappropriate	Possible	Possible
Good	Possible	Possible	Possible	Possible	Impossible	Possible	Possible	Possible
Good	Good	Possible	Possible	Possible	Possible	Inappropriate	Possible	Good
Possible on floors	Good	Good	Impossible	Good	Possible	Inappropriate	Possible	Good
Good	Possible	Possible	Possible	Good	Impossible	Good especially on the underside.	Possible	Possible
Good	Possible	Possible	Possible	Possible	Possible	Inappropriate	Possible	Possible
Good	Good	Inappropriate	Possible	Good	Impossible	Inappropriate	Possible	Possible
Good	Inappropriate	Inappropriate	Good	Good	Impossible	Inappropriate	Possible	Possible
Good	Possible	Possible	Good	Good	Possible	Impossible	Possible	Possible
Good	Good	Good	Good	Good	Impossible	Good with spray paints	Possible	Possible
Good	Inappropriate	Inappropriate	Possible	Good	Good	Good	Possible	Possible
Good	Inappropriate	Inappropriate	Possible	Good	Impossible	Impossible	Possible	Possible
Good	Inappropriate	Inappropriate	Possible	Good	Impossible	Good	Possible	Possible

Preparing to Paint

CHARGED-UP WITH enthusiasm for your project it can be very frustrating to have to start preparing your wall or furniture when all you want to do is get on with it. A too meticulous approach can mean that all the fun is removed but a too lackadaisical approach may result in shabby work which does not last. As with everything, moderation is the answer.

Before painting walls, make certain that the surface is clean and grease free, especially around doors. Cracks are the major repair necessary on the wall and these must be filled and rubbed back so that they are completely even and flat.

With furniture, old coats of wax, varnish, or paint need to be removed, as they can become very unstable when painted over. Varnishes and paints are usually easy to remove with a commercial paint stripper, although old oil paints can be arduous to strip. Waxes are cleared in a similar way, using a commercial wax remover. The stripped furniture should be rubbed back with some coarse sandpaper, making a good key for the fresh paint to adhere to.

Missing pieces of veneer or holes and cracks in wood need to be filled with a commercial filler. A very deeply-grained wood should be filled, especially if you are planning to use a technique which specifies the need for a smooth surface.

Remember that proper preparation prevents the decorative paint finish being interfered with by the woodwork or wall underneath. Prepare the basic surface as much as is necessary but don't let it spoil your enjoyment of the painting.

FILLING CRACKS
1 Lay a generous amount of commercial filler over the crack using a trowel.

2 Use the flat edge of the trowel to work the filler into the crack. Pull the trowel down to make a smooth surface. Leave to dry, following the manufacturer's instructions.

3 Sand the wall using fine-grade sandpaper. Wrap the paper around a wooden block for ease of use. Brush off all the dust before applying your base coat.

STRIPPING PAINT AND VARNISH
1 Commercial paint strippers are highly caustic so always wear protective gloves. Use an old paintbrush to apply the stripper and leave it on until the old coat begins to bubble up.

2 Remove the softened paint or varnish with coarse steel wool. Do not allow the stripper to dry or you will have difficulty removing it. Wipe off excess stripper and paint or varnish particles with a damp cloth.

REMOVING WAX

1 Soak some very fine steel wool in commercial wax remover and rub it over the surface. Wax remover dries quickly so tackle a small area at a time and do not let the steel wool dry out.

2 While the surface is still wet, use a soft cloth to wipe away any remnants of wax, dirt, or wax remover.

FILLING HOLES

1 Fill holes in furniture with a commercial filler, using a trowel to apply it. Lay a thin layer and leave to dry, following the manufacturer's instructions.

2 Paint the surface with a water-based paint. A flat paint will reveal any surface unevenness and indicate areas which still need filling. Fill these in the same way and leave to dry.

3 Sand the surface well with a medium-grade sandpaper. Wrapping the paper around a block makes it easier to handle. Paint and rub down the surface once more.

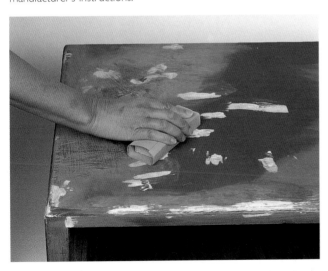

Protecting the Surface

WALLS AND WOODWORK with a paint finish do not need to be protected with varnish, except where they are in vulnerable positions such as stairways, halls, and kitchens, when the most they will need is a matt or mid-sheen/satin varnish. Otherwise, the glazed surface alone is protected enough. Furniture generally does need protecting with varnish or wax, as it is more likely to be frequently handled and sometimes knocked.

Clear varnishes and waxes can darken, or at best slightly alter, the colour of painted finishes so it is a good idea to check the result by testing before you start.

You can use varnish to your advantage for decorative reasons as well as protection, such as to give the surface a high shine, a matt look, or an aged effect. A high shine on rich dark colours looks wonderful and gives the colours vivacity and depth. Gloss varnish over stone faux finishes and mid-sheen/satin varnish on wood effects actually add to the authenticity of the finishes. A matt varnish looks good with chalky or pastel colours where protection is needed without it showing. However, matt varnish is not very strong so you may want to protect with gloss varnish first and finish with matt varnish.

Waxes are used more for the soft, mellow finish they impart than the strength of their protection. The solvents in the wax penetrate the surface to give it strength, so wax must be applied to absorbent surfaces. Shiny surfaces such as gloss varnish, plastic, or metal, will reject the solvents.

ABOVE *A mid-sheen/satin varnish (also called semi-gloss) is between matt and gloss in look, and has been applied to this moulding over a paint finish. This varnish is water-based with an acrylic base. It is quick-drying and completely colourless and odourless. An oil-based varnish will have a similar effect but will take longer to dry and gives the surface a slight yellow tone which emphasizes and deepens the colours.*

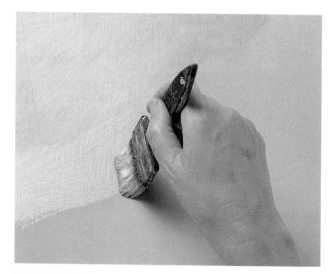

APPLYING VARNISH

Apply a thin, even layer of varnish using a flat varnish brush. Spread the varnish out with the tip of the brush. Try not to overbrush, which will cause streaking marks. On a wall use as large a brush as you can handle and work in a systematic way that prevents you from applying wet varnish to an already dry patch; this will alter the look of the varnish.

COLOURING VARNISH

To obtain more depth, or change the tone of your effect, a varnish can be coloured. While the varnish is still wet, dip your varnish brush into some powder pigment or sprinkle the pigment directly on to a horizontal surface. A little pigment often goes a long way so use it sparingly until you understand the pigment's strength.

LEFT *Clear wax imparts a soft, attractive sheen which is in between the dead flat effect of matt varnish or the shiny appearance of gloss and mid-sheen/satin varnishes. Wax is not as protective as varnish and so is used for its finish and on items which do not get a tremendous amount of wear and tear.*

LEFT *Dark wax imparts its colour on to the surface and is useful for creating an aged or antiqued look. To accentuate the aged look dark wax can be applied to moulded objects and allowed to settle in the crevices, as here, simulating the accumulation of grime over the years.*

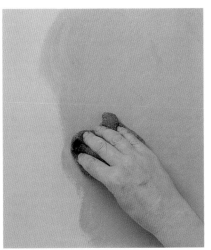

APPLYING WAX

1 Use very fine steel wool to apply a generous amount of wax to the surface, rubbing it in gently. The surface being waxed should be absorbent, so that the solvents in the wax can sink into it, giving it strength.

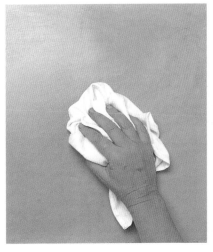

2 When the surface is dry it will no longer be tacky to the touch and the wax can be polished with a soft, clean cotton cloth. This action will produce a high sheen which can be maintained by polishing with beeswax three or four times a year.

COLOURING WAX

A clear or neutral wax can be coloured with pigment. Mix the pigment in with a palette knife until you have the desired intensity. The coloured wax is applied in the same way as Steps 1–2 above. This means you can make as many different-coloured waxes as you like from natural browns to brilliant blues.

CHAPTER III

BASIC FINISHES

The basic finishes are very versatile, and can be used on walls, woodwork, or furniture. For each the principle is to break up a coat of coloured glaze with brushes, rags, combs, or sponges to reveal the base colour.

Mutton Clothing

UTTON CLOTHING GIVES a fine and delicate finish of very tiny flecks of paint, and is less robust than many of the other paint finishes. A paint and glaze mixture is applied over a base coat and lifted off with a mutton cloth, leaving an impression of the weave behind it and the base colour showing through. It has a rather gentle, cloudy look because the mutton cloth absorbs more glaze in some areas than in others.

Mutton cloth, also known as stockinet, was originally used by butchers for wrapping meat, but is now more commonly used for cleaning. It can be bought in hardware stores, decorating shops, and car accessory shops. Use cotton mutton cloth which absorbs glaze well, rather than the nylon variety.

The mutton cloth is folded to make a firm pad, and frayed edges are tucked into the middle. To minimize the number of loose threads, do not cut the piece of mutton cloth with scissors but pull a continuous thread until it snags and you can tear the cloth apart. The size of the mutton cloth pad will affect the kind of mark you make; a large pad will leave a more generous mark, a small pad will give a tighter, more controlled feel. After a while the pad will become saturated with glaze and cease to make any impression. In fact, it will start to put glaze back on rather than taking it off. Unfold and refold the mutton cloth, leaving a clean pad to continue working with. When the whole cloth is wet, form a new pad with a fresh piece of mutton cloth.

Because mutton cloth absorbs a lot of glaze, the base colour in this finish is dominant, and therefore very important. If a very pale colour or white is used for the base then the finished effect will be light. For a strong effect a mid-tone hue should be used as the base coat for a darker glaze.

You can create a rich effect by painting and mutton clothing two or more layers on top of each other. However, if you add too many coats the base coat will be obliterated and the overall effect will lack depth and cease to have a light, airy look.

Mutton clothing can be a good alternative to stippling (see pp. 54–55) as it has the same fine speckled surface but it is more uneven than stippling.

SUITABILITY
Walls, ceilings, and furniture, particularly large pieces.

DIFFICULTY
*

MATERIALS
Glaze • Paint

EQUIPMENT
Household paintbrush, for applying glaze
Mutton cloth
10 x 2.5cm (4 x 1in) stippling brush,
for corners and cornices

POINTS TO CONSIDER
- A large wall can use up quite a lot of mutton cloth. It is advisable to prepare a pile of mutton cloth pads in advance.
- Remember to tuck in the edges of the cloth to avoid lose threads sticking to the glaze.

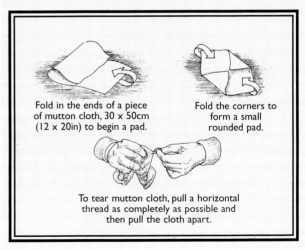

Fold in the ends of a piece of mutton cloth, 30 x 50cm (12 x 20in) to begin a pad.

Fold the corners to form a small rounded pad.

To tear mutton cloth, pull a horizontal thread as completely as possible and then pull the cloth apart.

LEFT AND OPPOSITE *The finish in this hall is a variation of simple mutton clothing. Whilst dabbing, the pad has also been twisted to create swirls of pattern. The vibrant colour provides a strong contrast to the marbled dado.*

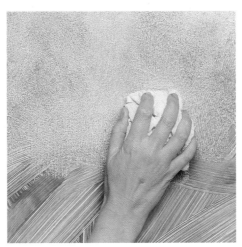

1 Paint the glaze evenly and thinly over the base coat. If it is too thickly applied the mutton cloth will not have enough impact and become saturated too quickly.

2 Fold the mutton cloth into a pad and use a swift, firm dabbing action to lift the glaze off. It is possible, with practice, to achieve a completely even look.

TOP
Mid-blue on
yellow ochre

MIDDLE
Greyed blue
on pale,
green-blue

BOTTOM
Warm blue
on plaster
pink

Ragging

RAGGING IS ONE OF the best-known decorative finishes, for several reasons. It is adaptable, quick and easy to execute, and needs no specialist tools. It can look soft, delicate, and subtle or deep and intense depending on the choice of colour combinations, the amount of glaze taken off with the rag, how the rag is held in the hand, and the type of rag used. If a room is ragged by several different people there will often be a marked difference in the finished effect.

The coloured glaze is applied over a dry base coat in small patches of about 50cm (20in) square. A piece of cloth, also 50cm (20in) square, is crumpled up loosely and dabbed on to the wet glaze, lifting it off in places to reveal the colour beneath. As the rag absorbs the glaze it needs to be re-formed to avoid dabbing glaze back on to the surface.

When the first coat is dry a second or even third coat can be applied in different colours. If too many coats are applied, however, some of the depth will be lost. The standard style of ragging is to use a glaze colour that is a few tones darker than a pale background. It is usual to rag until there are no brush-marks visible, but they can be left to make a feature.

Ragging is usually done with a soft cotton, or mainly cotton, cloth. Different rags can make quite a difference in the appearance and effect of the technique so, before you start, make sure you have a sufficient store of the same type of rag to enable you to complete a whole room. Old sheeting is ideal, and old clothes are also good as long as they have sufficient cotton in them. Anything with too much nylon, or a shiny cloth, will not be absorbent enough and you will end up putting more glaze on than you are taking off. Anything woolly or with a pile may shed fabric on the work and so should be avoided. Try dishcloths and fabrics with a prominent texture. Other possible materials include plastic bags, paper bags, and chamois leather. Plastic or strong paper makes very striking, definite marks. Dampened chamois leather absorbs a lot of glaze and makes a pronounced effect with strong contrasts.

The technique of ragging a large area is most easily executed by two people working together, although it is quite possible to do it on your own. The first person applies the glaze fairly generously, starting at the ceiling and working in patches down the wall. The second person rags in the first patch leaving a strip of unragged glaze around the edge so that the first person can work back into the wet glaze. Working in this way ensures there will be no dark line left where glaze has not been ragged because it has begun to dry.

SUITABILITY
Everything, including walls, ceilings, floors, and furniture.

DIFFICULTY
**

MATERIALS
Glaze • Paint

EQUIPMENT
Household paintbrush, for applying glaze
Cotton cloth, for standard look, torn into 50-cm (20-in) square pieces. For an average room of about 3.75 x 4m (12 x 15ft) you will require the equivalent of a double sheet,
OR crinkled or inflated plastic bags,
OR dampened chamois leather.
10 x 2.5cm (4 x1in) stippling brush or household paintbrush, for corners and cornices

POINTS TO CONSIDER
- Take care not to apply too much glaze into the corners and ceiling of a room where the effect will be too dark.
- Don't rag into an area which has already been done as this may make the work uneven.
- Finish one wall at a time or one surface of a piece of furniture.
- Keep reviewing the work as you go along, so that the amount of glaze applied stays fairly consistent and does not become patchy in areas.
- Remember the effect is hand done and should not be too repetitive.

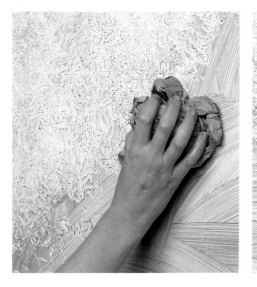

FAR LEFT *Ragging with a paper bag produces a less delicate finish because paper is not as absorbent as cotton.*

LEFT *Another effect can be created using a plastic bag. As plastic is non-absorbent it will quickly start to put glaze back on to the wall, so you will need a ready supply of bags.*

OPPOSITE *A room can be ragged quite quickly. It is a very adaptable technique, suitable for many different types of houses and interiors. It can also be used in conjunction with many other finishes and techniques, including stencilling.*

1 Cover the surface with a thin layer of glaze. Try not to build up too much glaze in the corners and edges, but make sure that the whole surface is adequately covered.

2 Lift the glaze off gently with a loosely-crumpled cotton rag. If the glaze has become too dry, you will need to apply more pressure. This should be avoided if possible.

3 As the rag becomes covered with glaze, refold it. Eventually, the rag will become soaked and will have to be discarded.

4 When the whole room has been ragged, any excess glaze that has built up along the edges or in corners can be evened out using a small stippling brush.

TOP
Yellow ochre on pale, warm brown

MIDDLE
Pale taupe on pale, warm brown

BOTTOM
Mid-green on pale, warm brown

Frottage

THIS TECHNIQUE RESULTS in a random, uneven painted effect. Frottage is the French word for 'rubbing' and the technique involves rubbing a sheet of newspaper over the wet paint mixture. The paper absorbs the mixture more in some places than in others, producing an irregular, random pattern. Each new sheet of paper and fresh layer of paint produces a different effect.

Frottage can be carried out using a mixture of paint, glaze, and a little water or simply using paint thinned with water. Without the glaze the contrast between the solid base coat and the thinned-paint top coat is not too obvious, giving a pleasingly subtle look. However, without the glaze the paint dries quickly leaving less time to work, therefore it is advisable to work in small areas at a time. When using the basic paint and water mix take care not to dilute the paint too much, since a runny consistency will leave visible drips on your surface.

The newspaper can be used flat to make large shapes or crumpled up to make a smaller design. Small lines are created by the 'grain' of the newspaper and these may begin to give a sense of direction to your overall effect. Use different sheets of newspaper and turn them around randomly to maintain an irregular feel. You can also tear up sections of newspaper into rectangles or strips to use in isolated areas or specific shapes.

Alternatively, use crumpled tissue paper for a smaller, more even pattern than newspaper, or a dampened length of fabric. The fabric removes a lot of colour making a dramatic, large pattern, so you may want to try applying a thicker layer of paint in the first instance. Fabric has the distinct advantage of being reusable. Once the fabric has absorbed a lot of paint – between two or three uses – it can be rinsed and squeezed out, ready for use again.

Use colours which are tonally similar for this technique. Too strong a contrast will result in an uncomfortably coarse effect. Several layers of colours can be used to build up a depth of colour and interest. Do not attempt to do this until the previous layer is completely dry.

SUITABILITY
Walls, floors, and furniture

DIFFICULTY
**

MATERIALS
Glaze • Paint • Water
OR
Paint • Water

EQUIPMENT
Household paintbrush, for applying paint mixture
Newspaper

POINTS TO CONSIDER
- The fold in a sheet of newspaper can make an annoying intrusion which repeats all over the surface. You can go over this with crumpled newspaper while the paint is still wet, or frottage another layer of colour once the first coat is completely dry.
- Avoid overlapping areas of glaze or thinned paint. This will result in a heavy line where each section joins.

1 Apply your paint, glaze, and water or diluted paint mix to a dry base coat, over an area slightly larger than a sheet of newspaper. Here, the technique is being carried out over a wall which has already been frottaged twice.

2 Place a sheet of newspaper over the wet paint, leaving a wet edge – a strip of wet paint untouched by newspaper. Smooth the newspaper out with your hands, applying varying amounts of pressure for unpredictable results.

3 Remove the newspaper quickly. To continue covering your surface apply another patch of thinned paint or glaze mixture, and position the newspaper over the new panel and the wet edge of the previous panel.

LEFT *Varying the pressure you use to rub the newspaper will produce different effects and taking note of the absorbency of the paper and the paint will help you to control the end result.*

BELOW *A warm, biscuit brown base coat has been frottaged using a lighter top coat colour. The soft, putty grey of the top coat contained a lot of opaque white and so it was necessary to add a little glaze to the paint to give it a translucent quality.*

TOP
Pale brown
on grey

MIDDLE
Off-white on
grey

BOTTOM
Pale yellow
then pale
brown on
pale mauve

Stippling

STIPPLING IS A VERY delicate and sophisticated finish, suitable for furniture, walls, and panelling. The finished effect is an even layer of very fine dots of glaze colour which allow the base colour to show through. From a distance the dotted effect cannot be seen, instead the colours merge. The stippling finish shows up any bumps or imperfections, so it is essential to begin with a smooth surface.

Once the glaze and paint mixture has been applied, the whole of the flat surface of the stippling brush is used to hit the surface. This stippling motion both lifts off and distributes the glaze colour. The stippling action must be done with a steady, firm motion. Hitting too hard makes the bristles bend and leaves scratchy marks, while not hitting hard enough will have little effect at all. It is also possible to work with the brush at an angle so that only part of the bristles are touching the surface. This results in a broken, randomly-speckled finish.

At first the brush takes off a lot of glaze mixture leaving a 'bald' patch on your work, so it is best to allow the brush to build up a little glaze on the bristles by stippling on a hidden surface or some scrap paper before starting. As you are working, the stippling brush will become saturated with glaze and should be wiped gently with a clean rag.

The idea of stippling is to remove all the brushmarks leaving a dry, very fine look. If too much glaze is applied in the first place then the stippling will result in a rather thick and wet look. If this happens, keep stippling and wiping the brush with a rag to remove the excess or begin again.

A wide range of stippling brushes is available, from ones with very firm closely-packed bristles which are good for work with oil-based glazes, to softer more loosely-packed bristles which are suitable for work with water-based glazes. There are also many sizes available Choose one appropriate in size to the area you wish to cover. An 18 x 12cm (7 x 5in) brush is useful for walls, while a 7.5 x 10cm (3 x 4in) brush is very practical for furniture. A 10 x 2.5cm (4 x 1in) brush is good for corners and small areas. Much larger brushes are also available. Wash the brush in water if it is to be left for any length of time to prevent the glaze mix drying on the bristles.

The stippling technique gives depth and brilliance to most strong or traditional colours. A bright and light colour used as a base will shine through the coloured glaze as if reflecting light. A strongly-coloured glaze needs a strong and bright base coat to give it the vitality it deserves. However, because stippling is an extremely delicate finish, it is not suitable for very pale colours which simply will not be seen.

Traditionally used in the 18th century, stippling looks good combined with dragging (see pp. 64–66) on panelling or used on a dado with dragging above. Panels can be aged by stippling a darker colour at the edges and corners.

SUITABILITY
Walls and furniture (large and small).

DIFFICULTY
**

MATERIALS
Glaze • Paint

EQUIPMENT
Household paintbrush, for applying glaze
Stippling brush, size appropriate to work

POINTS TO CONSIDER
- Use a stronger coloured glaze than you think necessary. The stippling finish tends to make colours appear lighter than their original.
- If your surface is not sufficiently smooth for stippling, you will find that mutton clothing makes a very good alternative (see pp. 48–49).

---

1 Cover the surface with a thin layer of glaze. Dab a stippling brush firmly and evenly over the surface to lift the glaze. Once the glaze is drying, it is difficult to remove scuffs and splashes so take care not to disturb previously finished areas. As the glaze builds up on the brush, wipe it off gently with a clean rag.

OPPOSITE *Stippling provides a good background in a room that has a lot of architectural detail and many pictures on the wall.*

OPPOSITE FAR RIGHT *Mouldings and carved objects look very effective when stippled. For added contrast the glaze on the raised areas can be wiped off with a cloth.*

ABOVE *Stippling has a very even finish which, from a distance, can look almost flat. It nevertheless has a mysterious quality and depth; flat paint appears quite dead by comparison. Here, the bright base coat gives the stippling a vibrant quality.*

TOP
Yellow on
pale green

MIDDLE
Warm
brown on
pale green

BOTTOM
Warm blue
on pale
green

Rag Rolling

THIS FINISH IS A sophisticated adaptation of ragging. It involves three different stages: the glaze is brushed on with a household paintbrush, dabbed firmly with a stippling brush, and then rag rolled – a lightly-crumpled cotton cloth is rolled up the surface.

All three stages have to be completed before the glaze becomes too dry, so large areas are best undertaken by at least two, possibly three, people – one to apply the glaze, one to stipple it, and one to rag roll. One person alone can tackle panels or small areas such as furniture surfaces.

Once the glaze has been stippled, you can rag roll heavily or lightly, according to the effect you want to create and how much of the stipple you wish to leave revealed. A very lightly-rolled rag using soft colours gives a delicate, sophisticated look. Contrary to popular belief, the rag should not be folded into a sausage shape, but simply crumpled and then rolled upward. A sausage shape will make a strong, specific pattern which repeats for a time but cannot be maintained when the sausage is re-formed as it becomes saturated with glaze.

The colour of the base coat is more important with this technique than with any other. The rolled rag reveals a lot of base colour which may look too stark in contrast to the more densely-coloured stipple.

As rag rolling is a combination of stippling and ragging, much of the advice for both these techniques applies (see pp. 50–51 and 54–55). Aim for an all-over evenness; this depends on the even application of paint and a steady hand with the stippling brush, and rag.

SUITABILITY
Large areas such as walls, panels, and larger pieces of furniture.

DIFFICULTY
***

MATERIALS
Glaze • Paint

EQUIPMENT
Household paintbrush, for applying glaze
Stippling brush, size appropriate to work
Cotton cloth, for an average room of about 3.75 x 4m
(12 x 15ft) you will require the equivalent of a double sheet.

POINTS TO CONSIDER
- Re-form the rag frequently to stop it forming into a sausage shape and making unwanted, regimented patterns.
- Don't allow the stippled glaze to dry before rag rolling.

1 Cover the surface in a thin layer of glaze. Dab a stippling brush firmly and evenly over the surface to lift the glaze. Use a brush appropriate to the size of the surface.

2 While the glaze is still wet, roll a crumpled rag up the wall, taking care not to slip or to make a pattern that cannot be repeated because it is too regimented.

ABOVE *How lightly or heavily you rag roll the wall after stippling is a matter of personal taste. Here, the wall has been rag rolled fairly lightly to leave quite a lot of the stipple revealed.*

OPPOSITE *The whole chest of drawers was stippled and only the drawers rag rolled. You can see the characteristic texture achieved by rag rolling, which resembles crumpled fabric.*

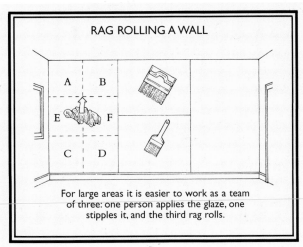

RAG ROLLING A WALL

A   B

E   F

C   D

For large areas it is easier to work as a team of three: one person applies the glaze, one stipples it, and the third rag rolls.

TOP
Yellow ochre
on pale,
grey-green

MIDDLE
Green-blue
on pale
yellow

BOTTOM
Greyed
brown on
earth pink

Sponging On

SPONGING ON IS ONE of the quickest finishes to achieve as it involves only one stage. It is also a finish that can be used on uneven surfaces such as woodchip or other raised wallpapers. The sponge is dipped in the paint and glaze mixture and dabbed lightly several times over the surface to produce an informal, speckled effect.

Natural marine sponges are usually used as they produce interesting and irregular marks. Each one is quite different, giving larger or tighter spotty designs. These natural sponges are not cheap and are sometimes hard to find in a good, workable size. Synthetic sponges that imitate the holey characteristic of natural ones may be used instead. They are usually rectangular so you should think about incorporating the straight edges into the design.

Before you start, squeeze out the sponge in clean water to soften it and make it pliable. The paint and glaze should be mixed in a large container and then a small amount transferred to a paint tray. Dipping the sponge into the thin layer of glaze in the tray ensures it does not become saturated: a saturated sponge will make heavy, thick impressions and lose definition. The first dab of the sponge may make larger and more obvious speckles than subsequent prints, because of the amount of glaze on the sponge. To avoid this inconsistency, dab excess glaze on to some scrap paper before you begin.

The difficulty of this technique lies in covering an area without establishing a pattern that looks either too obvious or too irregular. Step back frequently from your work and look at it from a distance to see the effect that is being made. It is also a good idea to move the sponge slightly when working, to avoid defining the individual round shape of the sponge and making a regular pattern.

With this technique it is particularly important to use colours in closely-related tones, to avoid crude and heavy-handed freckles. There are, of course, exceptions; a black base with white sponging can look dramatic and very effective, especially in small areas.

Two or more colours can be applied over the base colour to give variation, interest, and depth. These colours must be carefully chosen as it is very easy to end up with discordant hues and an unbalanced and overworked result. Using too many colours with a marked difference between the tones is a common mistake. The colours can be applied at the same time, working with either several sponges or with different parts of the same sponge, but by using this method you run the risk of the wet colours mixing and becoming dirtied. Alternatively, you can sponge on one colour, leave it to dry, and then sponge on another. This has the advantage of keeping each colour clean and separate from the others.

You can use sponging on over sponging off (see pp. 60–61). Sponging on is used in making a granite and stone work finish, and can also be used in the marbling technique (see pp. 99, 132–133, and 79).

SUITABILITY
Everything, including walls, ceilings, floors, and furniture.
Unsatisfactory on carved items.

DIFFICULTY
***

MATERIALS
Glaze • Paint

EQUIPMENT
Natural or synthetic sponge
Paint tray

POINTS TO CONSIDER
- No natural sponge is exactly like another, so expect different results if you use different sponges.
- To keep a favourite sponge in good condition wash out all the glaze mixture with water and soap and allow it to dry.
- Whilst it is fine to layer the effect using several tones of a single colour, you should not produce more than three layers which will inevitably result in a discordant mess.
- If yellow is sponged over a blue base coat, the blue will 'shine' through the yellow. From a distance this will take on a greenish appearance.

1 Mix your paint and glaze in a large paint kettle and pour a small quantity into a paint tray. Squeeze the sponge out in clean water and dip it lightly into the paint tray.

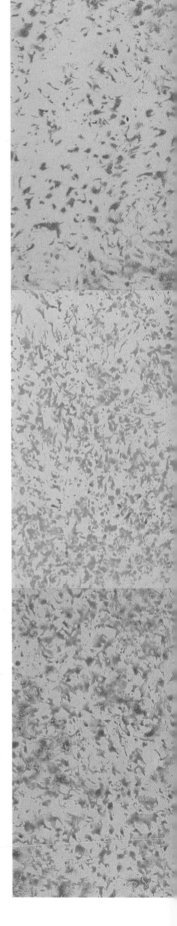

2 Having dabbed excess glaze on to some scrap paper, dab the sponge gently on your surface. Try to vary the pressure you exert on the sponge.

3 The effect can be varied by leaving larger spaces between the sponge marks and applying a second colour in the gaps. Keep base and glaze colours close in tone.

4 You can achieve numerable variations by experimenting with sponging additional colours over dry glaze coats. Remember that the final colour will be dominant.

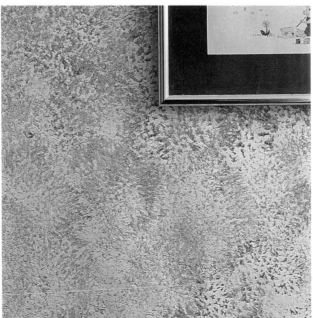

RIGHT *A deep red glaze was sponged over an off-white base coat to create a bright, dramatic effect on a dining room wall.*

TOP
Terracotta
on mid-blue

MIDDLE
Turquoise
and terra-
cotta on
light blue

BOTTOM
Warm blue
and terra-
cotta on
mid-blue

Sponging Off

SPONGING OFF PRODUCES a casual, informal finish which is a little subtler than sponging on (see pp. 58–59). The paint and glaze mixture is applied with a household paintbrush and then lifted off with a dampened sponge, allowing the base colour to show through. Natural marine sponges are usually used, although a synthetic sponge with holes cut into it can be very effective.

The finished result can be spotty, flowery, or cloudy depending on how the sponge is handled and the shapes that are inherent within the sponge. Swirling the sponge lightly as it is applied to the wall gives the effect a sense of movement and liveliness.

Take care to ensure the sponge is neither too wet nor too dry before you apply it to the glazed surface. If it is too wet it will leave unsightly drips on your work, but if the sponge is too dry it will not pick up enough glaze. The sponge also needs to be dabbed confidently and positively, not tentatively.

As you work the sponge will become clogged with glaze and no longer be absorbent. At this point it is necessary to wash the sponge out completely in water and dishwashing liquid.

Use base and glaze colours that are close in tone, otherwise the finished result will look crude and dissonant. To achieve a finish with great depth, several colours can be applied one over the other. This is usually done by using the two sponging techniques together. After the surface has been sponged off it is then sponged on in either the same colour in a different tone or a different colour of the same tone. It is usually better to allow each layer to dry before applying the next, because wet colours will blend, possibly making a dirty colour or an unwanted third colour. Also, any mistakes can easily be wiped off a dry first layer without affecting it.

Sponging off is also used as part of the marbling and bird's eye maple woodgraining techniques (see pp. 81 and 115).

SUITABILITY
Everything, including walls, ceilings, floors, and furniture.

DIFFICULTY
***

MATERIALS
Glaze • Paint

EQUIPMENT
Household paintbrush, for applying glaze
Natural or synthetic sponge

POINTS TO CONSIDER
- Removing the glaze mixture is particularly difficult in the corners of a room or edges of panels. In these areas apply the glaze thinly and use a small piece of broken-off sponge.
- Apply the glaze in small areas at a time, panels no wider than a comfortable arm's reach are ideal. Leave a strip of unsponged glaze around the edge of the panel to work the next area of glaze into.

1 Apply a thin coat of glaze with a household paintbrush to cover the surface evenly. Work on small areas at a time so that the glaze remains wet and workable.

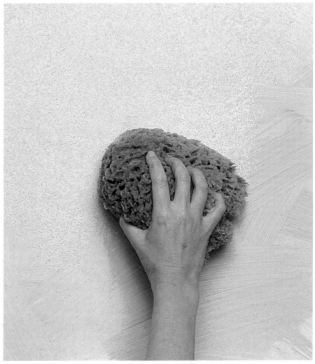

2 Squeeze out the sponge in water and dab it evenly on the surface to lift the glaze. When it is saturated wash the sponge in water and dishwashing liquid. Rinse.

3 You can vary the look by sponging off over a surface that has previously been sponged in a different colour. These techniques allow scope for experimentation with colour, tonal variation, pressure on the sponge, and different base coats, to achieve a wide range of effects.

BELOW *Over a yellow base, a varied glaze of bright red to deeper red was applied and then dabbed with a dampened sponge. When this was dry, a little yellow glaze was sponged on (see pp. 58–59) in parts to add highlights.*

TOP
Yellow on sand

MIDDLE
Green-blue on sand

BOTTOM
Pale terra-cotta and cool brown on sand

Colourwashing

COLOURWASHING IS a relaxed and generally informal technique which looks effective in both natural, earthy hues and stronger colours too. This is a good finish for undulating walls with an uneven surface because any imperfections will usually merge into the effect.

In this technique the coloured glaze is applied and gently wiped off, blended, and spread over the surface in all directions. This results in large and small sweeps of colour in various tones which allow the base colour to show through.

The glaze can be manipulated using a variety of tools and a range of movement styles. A piece of mutton cloth, a cotton rag, or a paintbrush can be used. The mutton cloth gives a very soft look with no brushmarks apparent while working with a brush gives a dramatic and dynamic look. The glaze mixture can be wiped off with long sweeping movements, perhaps for a large room or where strong colours are being used, or in a smaller tighter manner for a small room. For a traditional colourwash a wide variety of marks in all directions, lengths, and with softer and harder pressure exerted at varying intervals needs to be used, so that a regimental pattern is not established. Alternatively a pattern can be deliberately made of wavy or vertical lines.

The work of wiping off should be started when the glaze mixture is beginning to dry. If the mixture is too wet the glaze is too easily wiped away and you are left with coarse lines of colour. When the glaze is beginning to dry it is easier to apply various amounts of pressure to the surface so that softer and more varied sweeps of colour can be achieved. The colourwashed surface can be given more depth by repeating the technique with further layers of colour, once each previous coat is thoroughly dry.

SUITABILITY
Walls, ceilings, floors, and large areas of
furniture such as tabletops.

DIFFICULTY
***

MATERIALS
Glaze • Paint

EQUIPMENT
Household paintbrush, for applying glaze
Large household paintbrush, cotton rag, or mutton cloth

POINTS TO CONSIDER
- Wait for the glaze to dry a little before wiping it off. This will make it easier for you to apply varying degrees of pressure to the surface, giving the final effect more variety.

LEFT *Three glaze colours – dark red, blue, and a mix of the two – were colourwashed in patches over a pale blue-grey base coat to give this simple fireplace depth and interest.*

1 Apply a thin coat of glaze to the wall, brushing it out very thinly.

2 With a large, dry brush, wipe off the glaze in broad and sweeping strokes.

3 A dry cotton rag may be used as an alternative for wiping off the glaze. This produces a gentler effect. You can take off more or less of the glaze by applying varying degrees of pressure to the rag.

RIGHT As it is a loose and informal finish, colourwashing is a good solution in a country house where the plaster walls are uneven. It can provide a good background for additional decoration such as stencilling or printing.

TOP
Yellow ochre
on white

MIDDLE
Pale brown
on white

BOTTOM
Terracotta
on grass-
green

Dragging

RAGGING DERIVED FROM woodgraining techniques in the mid-18th century and produces a variegated, stripy effect. A brush with long bristles is pulled in a straight line – usually vertically but horizontally and diagonally also work well – across the wet glaze and paint mixture.

The glaze is applied thinly, in strips, down the surface. The tip of the dragging brush is placed at a close angle to the surface and pulled up and down over the glaze repeatedly. The up-and-down movement of the brush breaks up strong stripes, avoiding accurate vertical and continual lines which are very difficult to maintain across a whole surface. Glaze is not applied directly into corners or edges, instead the movement of the dragging brush will distribute the glaze into these areas. The brush will become saturated from time to time so wipe it on a rag to remove excess glaze.

As well as the long-bristled dragging brush, the flogging brush, which has even longer bristles, can also be used. Both brushes have bristles which are not only long but coarse and loosely packed. This allows them to break up the glaze into stripes, and then further into broken stripes. A cotton cloth dipped in glaze can also be used for dragging, producing soft stripes which blend together like watercolour. This alternative technique can only be used on short lengths of surface, like a piece of furniture, because you must drag in one continuous line without stopping: stopping and starting will leave an obvious and uncomfortable mark.

Two or more colours can be dragged over one another to create interesting variation and depth. Each layer should be dry before the next is applied and less colour should be applied for each subsequent layer, so that the previous colour is not obliterated. The tones of the base and glaze coats should be close, so the contrast is not jarring. For a classical look, use a pale sage-green over darker green, or a drab colour over a sand base coat. A more contemporary look might have emerald-green dragged over an orange base or mauve dragged over chrome yellow.

To give a chequered or plaid effect the colours can be dragged first vertically then horizontally. You can also create a wild silk effect by dragging down and then lightly flicking the tip of the brush diagonally.

Because of its classic finish, dragging is often used in combination with stippling (see pp. 54–55), and in the 18th century would have been used on doors, panelling, dados, and all woodwork. There is a particular method for dragging doors (see p. 158), but for furniture and woodwork the general rule is to drag in the same direction as the wood grain.

SUITABILITY
Walls, all woodwork, and furniture, particularly large items.

DIFFICULTY
***

MATERIALS
Glaze • Paint

EQUIPMENT
Household paintbrush, for applying glaze
Dragging or flogging brush

POINTS TO CONSIDER
• Remember to avoid allowing a build up of glaze to occur at the edges of your surface, which will result in dark patches. Push the glaze into these areas with the dragging brush rather than applying glaze directly to them.

1 Apply a thin coat of glaze, brushing it on with an up-and-down movement rather than haphazardly as in other techniques.

2 Draw a dragging brush up and down the wall using reasonable pressure, keeping the brush strokes parallel. The mark is made by the tips of the bristles.

3 You may also drag with a crumpled cotton rag, by dipping it into the glaze and drawing it down the surface. This technique is most suitable for small areas.

ABOVE *This door was dragged in the traditional method, vertically and horizontally.*

RIGHT *A blue glaze was dragged over a lilac base. When dry, a green glaze was dragged thinly over the blue so as not to obliterate it.*

4 When working from the cornice, apply pressure to the end of the bristles with your other hand. This will release enough glaze to spread to the top of the wall.

TOP
Warm blue
on sand

MIDDLE
Pinkish-
brown on
sand

BOTTOM
Green on
sand

RIGHT *Dragging can be used on particular parts of a piece of furniture, such as the stiles, rails, and surround of this cabinet.*

BELOW TOP *Dirtied yellow was dragged horizontally, then pale blue was dragged vertically on the left and crimson on the right.*

BELOW BOTTOM *Dirtied yellow was dragged vertically, crimson was dragged horizontally, and then pale blue was dragged vertically.*

BELOW RIGHT *Green was dragged in one direction and red in the opposite.*

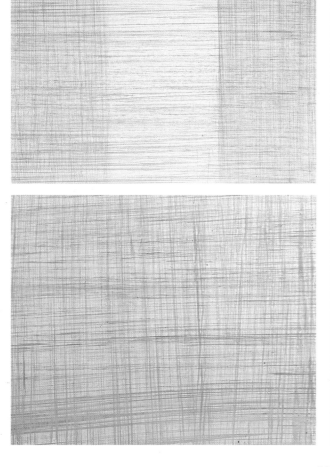

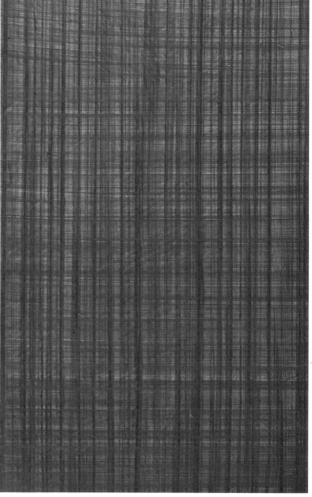

Flogging

THIS FINISH RESEMBLES a flecked version of the dragging technique (see pp. 64–66). The stripes of dragging are broken up, making lots of subtle, short lines. The technique is originally derived from oak graining and can be applied in brown colours to resemble wood, or executed in other colours for a decorative effect.

A fairly thin layer of glaze and paint mixture is applied in strips over the base coat. A flogging brush is used to drag the surface, spreading the glaze out evenly. The dragged finish is then hit quite firmly and repeatedly with the tip of the flogging brush, moving slowly upward. The hitting, or 'flogging', breaks up the lines of the dragging.

It is important to apply the right thickness of glaze. If the glaze is too thick and wet when it is hit with the flogging brush the appearance may be very crude and 'hairy'. If too thin and dry, the dragged lines will not be broken.

As with dragging, the tones of the base and the glaze colour should be close, to avoid a jarring contrast.

This finish can be painted anywhere, but it is quite time-consuming to flog walls. It is a suitable technique for furniture, panels, and architraves. The flogged finish is often used in combination with dragging.

SUITABILITY
Doors, particularly architraves, walls, dados, larger items of furniture, and frames.

DIFFICULTY
***

MATERIALS
Glaze • Paint

EQUIPMENT
Household paintbrush, for applying glaze
Flogging brush (size appropriate to work)

POINTS TO CONSIDER
• When the bristles of the flogging brush hit the glaze the very top of the brush will leave a line marked on the surface. By flogging upward you will cover this mark as you work.

1 Apply a thin coat of glaze to the surface and drag through it, using a flogging brush (see p. 64).

2 Starting from the base, hit the surface with the tip of the flogging brush, using a series of upward movements.

RIGHT *Flogging has been used in the panel, while the stiles have been dragged, in green over white. This effect has an unusual and contemporary look.*

TOP
Pale green-blue on yellow

MIDDLE
Brown ochre on grey

BOTTOM
Warm brown on grey

Combing

THE COMBING TECHNIQUE produces lines and stripes of different widths and so can be used to create a variety of decorative patterns. A comb with flat teeth is pulled across the wet glaze and paint mixture, lifting it off in parts.

Combs were originated for woodgraining, where they are used to simulate the grain of oak, but have also developed into a decorative tool used extensively in folk decoration. Of all the paint technique tools available the comb offers the most variety and allows the user to be creative.

There are two main types of comb commercially available, both made of a rubbery plastic. One is triangular in shape with each side offering teeth of different widths. The other has two edges, each with teeth graduating in size from quite fine to approximately 1.25cm (¹⁄₂in) in length. Larger, home-made combs can be cut out of rubberized floor tiles or cardboard using a sharp knife. Making your own comb will allow you to decide on the width and spread of teeth, and a large home-made comb will cover a wide area quickly. Only make the comb as wide as your two hands can hold, for ease of use.

Simple patterns can be made in a variety of ways. Wiggle or twist the comb as it is pulled down to make wavy stripes. Comb through the glaze first vertically and then horizontally to create a basic check. On a small area this can be done through a single layer of wet glaze, but on a wall or other large surface it is best to allow the stripes going one way to dry before reapplying the glaze and combing in the opposite direction. Combing can also be used quite simply to make a border along a frieze, dado rail, or around a door, although it is difficult to maintain the border in the same width.

You can use strongly-contrasting base and glaze coat colours for a vibrant or dramatic effect, or colours with little contrast to give a more subtle and mellow look. A second and even third glaze colour could also be applied and combed for a tartan weave effect. The final colour and the direction it was combed will be dominant, so think about whether you want a vertical or a horizontal look to your surface.

When working on a wall you will need to lift off and replace the comb as you reposition yourself. This action will leave a mark on the surface. If your base and glaze colours are close in tone this may not be noticeable, or you may decide that the mark becomes an integral part of your design. However, if the mark is unwanted it can be blended in carefully with a small brush. Also, when working on bumpy walls the comb will miss bits, but how much this matters depends on the effect you want to achieve.

SUITABILITY
Walls, floors, panels, furniture, and frames.

DIFFICULTY
***

MATERIALS
Glaze • Paint

EQUIPMENT
Household paintbrush, for applying glaze
Comb(s)

POINTS TO CONSIDER
- If the glaze mixture is applied too thickly the combing will cause a three-dimensional ridge to form.
- Hold on to the comb firmly as it may slip.

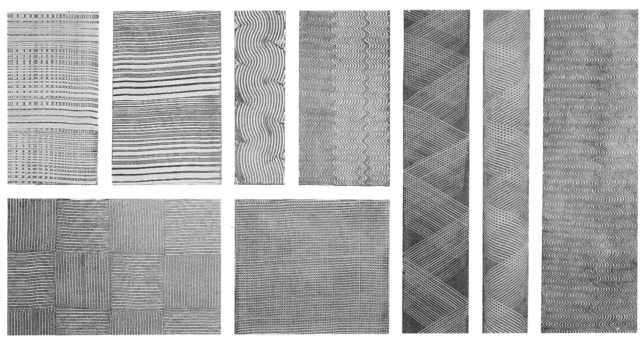

ABOVE *A myriad of patterns is possible, using both triangular and graduated combs. Here, before combing into red glaze over a white base coat, the glaze was mutton clothed (see pp. 48–49).*

1 Cover the surface with a thin and even layer of glaze. Using both hands, pull a graduated comb down carefully with an even pressure.

2 To make a chequered pattern, pull the comb horizontally through the wet glaze, holding it in both hands as before.

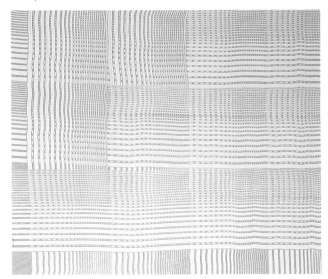

3 To introduce an element of variety to a chequered effect, turn the graduated comb round for alternate rows.

RIGHT *An attractive border or edging can be made by combing an undulating line. This gives a three-dimensional effect.*

RIGHT *The walls of this whole room have been combed horizontally, using a graduated comb, through brown-red glaze. A solid painted line indicates the dado rail and the door panels were treated with a heartgrainer (see p. 104).*

Spattering

SPATTERING IS THE FLICKING of paint, usually applied in two or three colours, on to a surface to produce small but varied spots. A paintbrush is loaded with diluted water-based paint and the handle hit with a stick, usually another brush, to throw the paint in a random but not uncontrolled manner on to the surface. Using a glaze mixture would make the paint thick and less inclined to flick off the brush.

A small amount of paint goes a long way in this technique, especially since it is mixed with water. How much water is added depends on the paint used. Artists' acrylics, for instance, need to be mixed with more water and for longer than low-vinyl paint or matt emulsion/flat latex. The final consistency must be thin enough to run slowly down the side of the container when the brush is wiped on the rim.

The brush retains far more paint than is apparent, so it is useful to test the spatter on scrap paper first, to dispel of excess paint. If the paint is too thick or too much is loaded on to the brush the result will be three-dimensional spots with blobs of paint raised above the surface. If the paint is the right consistency but there is too much on the brush then this can result in spots which are very large and difficult to control.

Use a brush with short bristles such as an artist's fitch. The bristles must be quite stiff so they can spring back when flicked. An old brush which has shed some of its bristles is often ideal. An alternative method, for a very fine spatter, is to use a small, short-haired brush and flick it by pulling your fingers quickly over the bristles.

The farther from the surface you hit your brush, the bigger your spots will be. So, for spots of the same size, flick your paint from the same place each time. Take care spattering small, round objects and those with acute angles because the paint flies past the surface and forms elongated splotches rather than spots. If you spatter densely or with earthy colours the effect can look traditional and reminiscent of stone or marble. Larger spots more loosely spaced can give a more contemporary look like a Jackson Pollock painting.

Think about the colours you are going to use before you begin. The colours could be different tones of the same hue or similar tones of different colours, with perhaps one brighter tone to lift the other colours.

The spattered effect is often done over a base of mutton clothing, ragging, or colourwashing (see pp. 48–51 and 62–63), since the well-defined spots are softened and given depth by a textured background. Bear in mind that spatters which have not gone to plan can be easily wiped off if the base coat is completely dry.

SUITABILITY
Walls, floors, furniture.

DIFFICULTY
****

MATERIALS
Water-based paint • Water

EQUIPMENT
Fitch or small, short-haired paintbrush
Stick or handle of another paintbrush

POINTS TO CONSIDER
- If you wish to contain the spattering within a certain area, use masking tape or scrap paper to cover the areas you do not want spattered.
- Test the consistency of the paint frequently, not just when you begin work.
- Take your time and do not try to rush the spatters.

1 To spatter a floor, half load a fitch with dilute paint and flick the brush from your wrist.

2 Spatter a second colour or tone in the same way. Although the effect is abandoned, the brush can be aimed precisely if the paint is the right consistency.

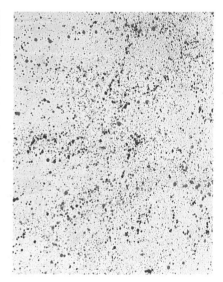

3 Vary the distance you spatter the paint from for a mix of different-sized spots.

4 For small spatter, mask any areas you do not want spattered with scrap paper or masking tape, and, holding the brush close to the surface, hit it against a stick.

5 For very fine spatter, flick the bristles back with your finger.

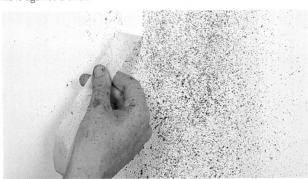

6 Spatter the surface fairly densely with three colours. Because there is no glaze in the spatter it takes a long time to dry so the different colours should be applied one after the other in the same painting session. When dry remove any masking tape.

LEFT *A bright red colour was used as the base colour then spattered with dark green, pale green, and dark red.*

BELOW *To spatter a large area relatively quickly and quite densely, a machine called a fuso can be used. It is filled with paint, held against the waist, and a handle turned to spatter the paint.*

TOP
Blue-black and red ochre on yellow colour-washed over white

BOTTOM
Blue-black and red ochre on grey colour-washed over white

CHAPTER IV

FAUX FINISHES

Inspired by natural materials – woods, stones, and shell – these techniques are designed to deceive the eye of the beholder into mistaking them for the real thing. The finishes can be produced as immaculate imitations or imaginative variations.

Marbling

THERE ARE MANY different types of marble and they vary enormously in both colour and design. Marble is found throughout the world, from North and South America and all over Europe, Africa, and parts of Asia. Marble is often used in building, so simulating it works well and can be extremely convincing.

Both colour and pattern vary enormously, from white and plain, like Carrara marble, to black streaked with white, and many marbles flecked and veined with numerous colours. There are marbles of every colour of the rainbow, including extraordinary colours like purple and vivid green, but the popular colours for both real and painted marble are warm greys, grey-blues, sienna yellows, and pale, rosy-pinks. Normally a fairly realistic marble is chosen to decorate a room, but some faux marbles, like folk-painted marbles, are deliberately exaggerated in colour and style.

Try to find a reference of the sort of marble you would like to achieve, or make a note of the specific colours and tones of a marble that stimulates you. This will enable you to establish its general characteristics and subtleties. It should be stressed, however, that the intention is not to copy the marble, which would be very difficult. Instead, what you are trying to achieve is a general idea, a summing up, a formalized way of presenting marble.

There are many different ways of achieving a marble look. In fact, there are probably as many different methods for marbling as there are marbles. The techniques can be carried out using either water-based or oil-based products. For hundreds of years oil-based products have been used because of their slow-drying time, but in recent years, a water-based glaze has been developed which dries relatively slowly. There are advantages and disadvantages with both methods. Oil-based glazes are still slower-drying than their water-based equivalent, allowing more time to work: once the coloured glaze is applied it can be manipulated for up to thirty minutes before it becomes unworkable. Water-based glaze dries in only ten to fifteen minutes, so you must be very confident with what you are doing. Oil-based products give off a strong turpentine smell, whilst water-based glazes are odourless. The choice is yours.

There are three stages involved in marbling: laying and softening a coat of glaze over a non-absorbent paint base, manipulating or distressing the glaze while it is still wet, and veining the marble after the glaze has dried. A marble can be left as it is at the end of each of the three stages, either simply as a glaze ground, as a distressed glaze ground, or a distressed glaze ground with veining. The most difficult task is the veining, and it is easy to go overboard and end up with too many heavy lines crossing over each other in the wrong places. Make sure the distressed glaze is completely dry before adding the veins, this way any unsuccessful veining can be wiped off without disturbing the work already done.

The shapes within a marble need to be composed to give the whole thing tension. Look at the negative shapes as well as the positive and think about drama, weight, and a sense of movement. The veins and spaces must not be equidistant nor should they be the same size. Colour and tone are all-important and it is common initially to use colours that are far too intense and too varied. If there is a sharp colour contrast, the finish appears to gain dimension and it ceases to give the impression of a completely flat surface. It is better to make a gentle marble than one that is too strident.

The final effect must be varnished (see pp. 44–45) to give it the look of real marble. It also feels more realistic if painted over a gessoed base (see pp. 140–141) which gives it the characteristic coldness of marble that is lacking if it is painted on wood or a plaster wall. However, this is a fine point. The most important thing for anyone to remember is that tonality is the all important consideration.

Imitation marble can be painted anywhere in a room, including the walls, floors, cornices, skirting-boards/baseboards, mouldings and architraves, and all furniture large or small. Floors look good made up into different patterns (see pp. 170–171), while large walls should be divided into slabs. Use a pencil to mark demarcation lines, leaving the lines on throughout, and do not marble in one long strip since this looks unrealistic. Marbled tabletops and small objects look wonderful, especially when a little wax is applied to soften the effect after varnishing.

Once you have discovered that you can successfully marble, do not go in for overkill. A simple combination of marbled skirting-board/baseboard and fireplace, or skirting-board/baseboard, dado, and architrave works very well.

SUITABILITY
Floors, walls, dados, architraves, skirting-boards/baseboards, bathroom furniture such as baths and bath-sides, tabletops, pillars, and small objects such as boxes and candlesticks.

MATERIALS
55% oil-based glaze
45% white spirit/mineral spirits
Artists' oil paint • Turpentine, to thin paint for veining
OR
Water-based glaze • Paint
Gloss varnish, oil- or water-based depending on which glaze was used.

EQUIPMENT
Household paintbrush or fitch, for applying glaze
Mutton cloth • Softening brush
Equipment for distressing could include rags, newspaper, cling film, natural sponge, or short-haired bristle brush.
Equipment for veining could include a feather, long-haired sable brush, or swordliner.
Varnish brush

POINTS TO CONSIDER
• Make the glaze coat varied by applying large and smaller areas of subtly-changing tones.

ABOVE *Baths and bathrooms are favourite areas for marbling because real marble is a popular architectural feature in the bathrooms of many grand houses. This bath has been marbled in one piece in several tones of raw umber. This has been echoed in grey and white above the mirror and on the cupboard door panels.*

LEFT *A simple wooden fireplace has been given a veined marble effect using first grey and then black veins over a lightly-softened grey glaze coat, on an off-white base.*

Sienna Marble

THIS MARBLE TECHNIQUE is carried out using different tones of a basic raw sienna glaze and paint mix. It can, of course, easily be adapted to recreate any marble colours. This marble technique can be followed omitting some of the later stages or using them all depending on the amount of activity needed for the project.

The Base Coat

Decide on the overall tone you want to achieve with the marble, whether this is light, dark, or medium, and apply a non-absorbent paint as a base coat accordingly: for the lightest result apply an off-white base coat and the darkest a pale, yellow ochre base coat. If working over wood, make certain the grain does not show through by painting several coats. Allow the base coat to completely dry.

The Glaze Coat

For the oil-based technique you need to mix the glaze with a lot of white spirit/mineral spirits, about 55% glaze to 45% white spirit/mineral spirits. Take one paint colour, in this case raw sienna, and mix it into the glaze to make two or three varying tones of a single colour. Adding more paint to the glaze will create a darker tone. Keep some of the paint unmixed, this will act as the darkest tone. When you become more adept with the technique and the use of colour then a wider range of hues can be tried, but it is best to keep them within the same range at first. About half the colour will be dabbed away during the process, so, at this stage, the colour will appear much darker and more intense than the end result.

When marbling a large surface, you will need to mix a lot of paint and glaze in one go: if you mix it in small amounts you will find that the colour is inconsistent each time you mix it.

To begin with, work in an area a little larger than this open book: if you attempt to work on a larger area you may find the glaze dries before you have a chance to manipulate it. As you become more proficient your working area will enlarge.

First thinly apply the lightest glaze mixture using a household paintbrush or a fitch – you need relatively little coloured glaze to cover the base coat. Use diagonal strokes to apply the glaze and leave some gaps. You should not be aiming for evenness or parallel strokes, but a feeling of a diagonal shift.

Apply the mid-tone glaze in a diagonal direction, filling in the gaps and lightly covering random patches of the previous glaze colour. Apply the darkest tone, the paint which has not been mixed with glaze, randomly and diagonally, but sparingly and in just a few places. Try to think of the marble you are painting as a panel that has been cut from a larger piece, with areas of colour that go off to other places. This effect can be achieved by painting the dark areas from the edges inwards, not just in middle. Aim for a soft, gently-changing surface with some lighter and some darker areas.

Mutton Clothing

After the glaze coat has been satisfactorily applied, and whilst it is still wet, it must be evened out using a mutton cloth to remove the brushmarks. At this stage you will need to work quickly and confidently. Before the glaze dries – this time will vary depending on atmospheric conditions and whether oil- or water-based glaze is being used – you need to mutton cloth, soften, and distress it.

Mutton clothing for all faux finishes takes a little practice. Fold the cloth into a pad (see pp. 48–49) and dab the surface firmly. Too much pressure removes too much glaze, while insufficient pressure does not remove enough. Do not go over the same area too often and if the glaze has started to dry you may need to be a bit more vigorous. This is a useful time to tone down any dark areas that are too accentuated.

Softening

It is necessary to soften the effect further using a badger-hair softening brush. The idea is to remove all stray brushmarks and any marks left by the fine weave of the mutton cloth. The finished result should be very smooth with a fine, even shine all over. This stage alone produces a satisfactory finished marble, but you could embellish it further with some of the techniques on the following pages.

1 Apply the lightest tone of glaze colour thinly and in a diagonal direction, leaving some random spaces. Working in a small area will allow you to manipulate the glaze before it dries.

2 Fill in the spaces with the mid-tone glaze, again in a generally diagonal direction. Lightly apply it in random areas over the lightest colour. Avoid making parallel diagonal stripes.

3 Add a few touches of the darkest tone, the paint without the glaze, also in a diagonal direction. Be careful not to overdo the darker areas.

4 At this stage you should already have established the underlying pattern of the basic ground coat. The stresses should be diagonal but not parallel. Be careful not to make this ground coat too complicated.

5 Firmly dab the wet glaze with a pad of mutton cloth to eradicate brushmarks. The cloth can also be used to lighten areas that are too dark.

6 Lightly brush over the surface with a softening brush. Let the movement of the brush come from your arm, not your wrist.

RIGHT
Three tones of grey on white

Distressing the Glaze

There are various ways to break up the glaze to give variation to the surface of the marble. You can spatter the surface with a dilutant – water, white spirit/mineral spirits, or turpentine – dab it with a dampened sponge or a rag, hit it with a rag, or manipulate it with cling film. You only need to use one of these techniques.

When distressing the glaze think about the design and shape you have already created with the glaze coat and continue working in the same diagonal direction.

When working with water-based glaze you may find that the glaze has dried before you have adequately distressed it. In this instance you can either sponge on a glaze mixture – using only a little glaze with the paint – or spatter paint over the surface (see pp. 70–71) to make freckles of colour. Alternatively a second coat of glaze can be applied and reworked, giving depth to your piece.

The final stage for each of the distressing methods is to soften the effect, using a softening brush. This will blend the effect into the background glaze.

SPATTERING DILUTANT
Dip a short-haired bristle brush in a small amount of dilutant – white spirit/mineral spirits or turpentine if you have been using oil-based glaze, or water if you have been using water-based glaze. Remove the excess by gently flicking the brush over scrap paper. Flick the brush over the glaze coat with your finger so that it is lightly spattered with dilutant. After a few seconds you will see spots start to appear. The more dilutant you have on the brush and the closer you are to the surface, the larger the spots will be. Do not add glaze to the dilutant since glaze acts like glue and will make the spots thick and lumpy. Brush over the effect with a softening brush.

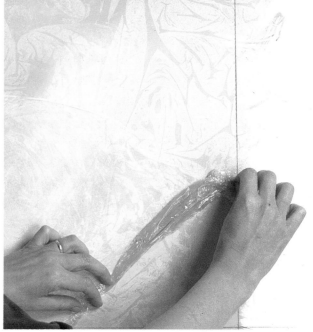

SHEET CLING FILM
This technique can have a rather alarmingly strident effect, particularly if the glaze is still very wet. Test the edge of the glaze with your finger to see how tacky it is. If it is very wet the cling film will remove a lot of glaze. If it is too dry the cling film will have no effect. When the glaze is just tacky, drop a sheet of cling film on the ground coat, blow on it, and gently lift it off. Use a softening brush to blend the effect. Where the effect is very strong use the softening brush to stipple (see pp. 54–55) and then soften again.

TWISTED CLING FILM
Twist a sheet of cling film and place it diagonally so that it lies in the general direction of the glaze coat, then lift it off. Try to avoid making a criss-cross pattern or producing parallel lines. Use a softening brush to blend the effect.

SPONGING OFF AND SPONGING ON

Wet a natural marine sponge in water and squeeze out well. Dab it evenly on the surface, in a diagonal direction, to lift off the glaze. Dip another sponge in a glaze mixture and dab the colour on to the surface, also in a diagonal direction. This is quite a dense effect and is most suitable for small objects and borders. When the sponged-on glaze has dried a little, soften lightly, using a softening brush, to take away the hard edges of the sponge pattern.

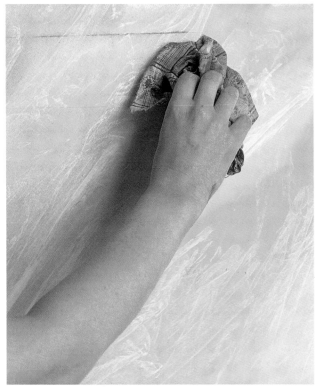

RAGGING

Scrunch up a rag so that it has angular folds. Lightly dab the rag over the still-wet glaze, working diagonally. Try not to create a series of parallel lines. Alternatively you can use newspaper. Use a softening brush to blend the effect.

HITTING THE GROUND

Take a long piece of dry rag. Hit your work diagonally in the general direction of the marble. This is good as an effect on its own or on other paint finishes. Soften lightly with a softening brush.

Veining

You can take your marble a stage further by veining, using different brushes and feathers to produce veins with different characteristics.

Veins can either be painted over a dry glaze coat or taken out of a wet glaze coat with a dilutant (the wetter the glaze, the more marked the effect). Veining on a dry ground allows you to wipe off mistakes. To create the effect you can use any long feather (goose feathers are traditional), a specialist brush called a swordliner, or an artist's sable brush with long hairs.

When painting on veins, use colours that vary only slightly in tone from the glaze coat, unless you are producing a specific marble (see pp. 88–89).

Vein in a diagonal direction following any darker or lighter areas. Some marbles have cross veins, but unless you are extremely competent at veining, do not attempt it. It is an individual characteristic of certain specific marbles and needs a good analysis of the tones involved. What you should be aiming for is a generalized marble effect with a summary of the characteristics – not a portrait of individual quirkiness.

FEATHER AND PAINT
Dip the angled end of a feather into some slightly thinned paint. Dab the feather on the dry surface and pull the feather down, to make both spots and veins. Soften with a softening brush.

FEATHER AND DILUTANT
Dip the feather in the dilutant (see p. 78) and shake off the excess. Pull and twist the feather over the wet glaze. Blend the veins using a softening brush.

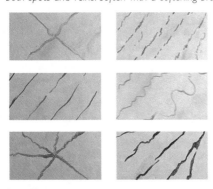

BAD VEINING
Although grossly oversimplified, parallel lines, wobbly veins, cobweb effects, and broken lines are very common faults.

GOOD VEINING
Although the vein may split at intervals to form quite complicated knots, two veins of the same tone never cross.

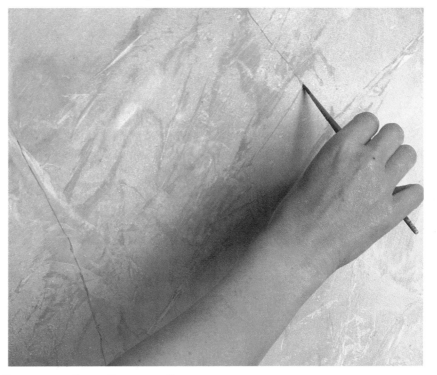

LONG-HAIRED SABLE BRUSH AND PAINT
Paint very fine lines over a dry glaze coat, using slightly thinned paint and a long-haired sable brush. Don't hold the brush like a pencil but hold it loosely and use only the very tip. Try to produce a line that varies in weight and character. Soften the effect.

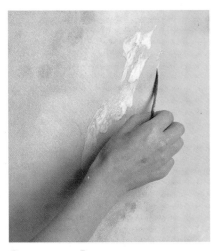

BRUSHES AND DILUTANT
Dip a swordliner (above) in dilutant. Use the very fine tip to make a line in the wet glaze. Twist the brush while it is on the glaze, then continue the line, again using the very tip.

Dip a long-haired sable brush (right) in dilutant and draw it over the wet glaze. Hold the brush loosely at the end.

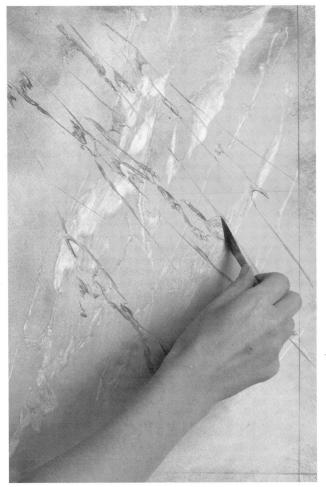

THIN VEINS
Paint fine veins using the thin side of a swordliner. Varying the pressure changes the thickness.

SWORDLINER AND PAINT
Use a swordliner with slightly thinned paint to draw veins. Using the broad side of the brush produces erratic marks which can be used in combination with finer lines. Soften the effect.

COMPLEX VEINING
Take out small areas in the centre of complex veining using a sable brush and a dilutant.

RIGHT
Raw sienna
on white

Marble Panels

Real marble is invariably used in panels or slabs. These slabs are often rectangular when on the wall and square when on the floor. Their size varies according to the dimensions of the room. Marble panels are not put up in steps like bricks, instead each slab is positioned directly above the one below and butted together without grouting.

To imitate marble panels first draw a grid across the whole surface. When working out what size to make the panels, think about how real marble was once used and recreate suitably-sized slabs. A soft pencil (3B) is ideal for delineating the slabs because it smudges slightly with the application of glaze, producing a more realistic line. The pencil line can be strengthened, if necessary, when the decoration is dry.

Each panel should then be marbled individually. Paint alternate panels, working around the room. Do not start to paint a panel next to one that is still wet and sticky, or your glaze will smudge and become muddy. After finishing each panel, wipe off any glaze that has spread on to the next slab.

To help bring the work together, it is best to do the veining when all the panels have been painted and are dry. The veining is generally all done in the same direction.

1 Prepare two glaze mixtures in different tones of the same colour.

2 Draw your panels in pencil on the surface. Apply the lightest tone in patches to the first panel, working diagonally. Fill in the gaps with the darker tone.

3 Soften and distress the panel (see pp. 77–79). You can vein at this point (see pp. 80–81) but you may prefer to wait until all the panels are completed. A coloured glaze may be applied over some of the dry panels to give them extra depth and variety.

4 Dab a pad of mutton cloth over the second glaze coat to eradicate brushmarks. Remove marks left by the weave of the cloth with a softening brush.

5 Repeat Steps 2–4 on alternate panels. Wipe clean the edges of the panels, along the pencil marks, using a mutton cloth or rag (right). When the panels are completely dry marble the adjacent slabs. Because the adjacent decoration is dry you can wipe the edges of each panel clean without disturbing the finish of the previous panel (above).

MARBLE PANELS

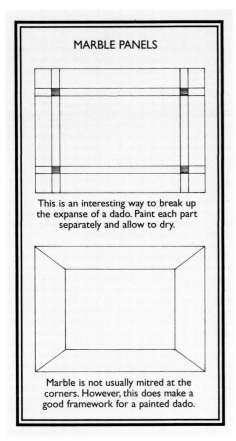

This is an interesting way to break up the expanse of a dado. Paint each part separately and allow to dry.

Marble is not usually mitred at the corners. However, this does make a good framework for a painted dado.

6 The pencil marks remain visible after painting, simulating the edges of real marble slabs. They may be emphasized when the glaze is dry. The veins should not flow from one slab to another.

TOP
Sienna glaze and raw umber veins on white, with a raw umber and white glaze applied over the top

BOTTOM
Pale sienna glaze and pale raw umber veins on white

Floating Marble

THIS TECHNIQUE EARNS its name from the way the paints and solvents float on the surface. It is an easy and light-hearted introduction to marbling and can be used to simulate real marble or simply to create a decorative effect.

The technique must be carried out on a horizontal surface. As with a straightforward marble, paint and glaze mixtures in two or three colours are applied over the base coat, dabbed with mutton cloth to obliterate brushmarks, and then softened. Next, a badger-hair brush – a round-ended one is best but a softening brush will also work – is dipped in water and the excess removed by dabbing the upright brush on some spare paper or cloth. The unique quality of the badger-hair brush means that when it is dabbed on the surface it produces many small spots. Dab the brush once to release the dots of water and then move on to the next space. When this action is then repeated using methylated spirits, the solvents cause the glaze to dissolve revealing the base in a series of spots. This initial 'spotting' using solvents is followed by a method of spotting using a little diluted water-based paint. For finer spots a little diluted paint can also be spattered over the surface to harmonize and merge the colours so that the effect does not look patchy.

Generally speaking, you should try to keep the base and glaze colours close in tone since a strong contrast between the spots and the overall colour will look very severe. A lot of the base colour is revealed through the spots and so needs to be considered carefully. For a strong effect the base coat should be dark or bright. An interesting and striking finish can be achieved by working with white glaze over a black base.

Floating marble can be applied in workable patches on a floor which can be squared up in pencil later (see pp. 172).

SUITABILITY
Any horizontal surface, such as floors and tabletops.

MATERIALS
Glaze • Paint • Water
Methylated spirits • Gloss varnish

EQUIPMENT
Household paintbrush or fitch, for applying glaze
Mutton cloth • Softening brush
Badger-hair brush, round-ended or softening
Fitch or small brush for spattering • Varnish brush

POINTS TO CONSIDER
- Be sparing with the paint in the paint and glaze mixture. Too much paint in the initial glaze will prevent the solvents from working.
- Remember that when using blue and yellow there will be a merging of colours resulting in areas of green.
- The diluted spattering paint should be thin enough to run slowly down the side of the container when the brush is wiped on the rim.

1 Apply two or three glaze colours in random patches all over the surface. The colours should be close in tone to the base coat. When working across a large floor it is best to split it up into comfortable working areas.

2 Dab a pad of mutton cloth over the entire area to eradicate brushmarks.

3 Soften lightly using a softening brush, to remove excess paint and mutton-cloth marks. This need not be too thorough.

4 Dip a round badger-hair brush in water. Remove the excess and dab on to the surface in patches. Repeat this action using methylated spirits and then using diluted paint.

5 If you cannot find a round badger-hair brush then a badger-hair softening brush will produce the same effect, but is not as easy to handle.

6 Load a small brush with diluted paint and flick the bristles with your finger to spatter the surface.

7 The pattern varies according to how much water and methylated spirits was initially dabbed on. The paint used for spotting dries at a different rate from the methylated spirits and patches of glaze, resulting in spots, lines, and rivulets of pattern. Varnish the effect (see pp. 44–45).

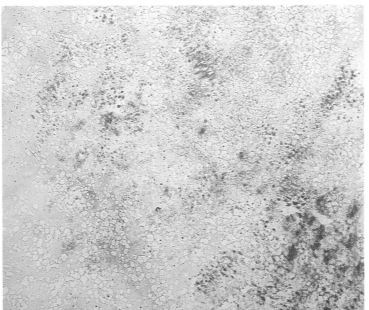

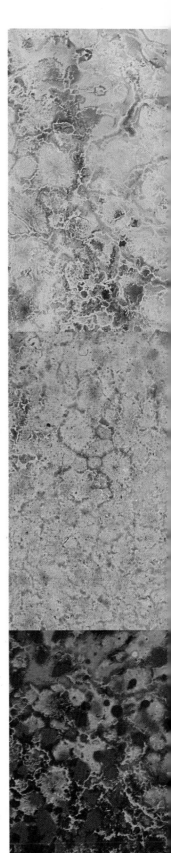

TOP
Blue and yellow ochre on white

MIDDLE
Green and terracotta on white

BOTTOM
Green and black on bright blue

Breccia Marble

THIS MARBLE IS made up of small or large pebble-like fragments, brought together to form particular patterns. Breccia Africano and Vert Antique (see p. 89) are two specific, better-known marbles of this class, but it is also possible to imitate the form of this marble more generally and using the colours of your choice.

Breccia is characterized by broken chunks of marble, which are imitated by wiping shapes out of the glaze coat with a rag. The general flow and design of the marble should be considered beforehand, and during its execution.

The size and feel of the marble can be altered according to the surface being painted. Large areas can accommodate big patterns of wide, spacious pebble shapes, combined with smaller shapes in some patches, while small objects are best decorated with thin, restricted patterns. The contrasts in the marble should be achieved by massing and sparseness, not by using strongly-contrasting colours.

Breccia marble is very quick-drying because the glaze is applied very thinly. Like all painted marbles, it should be varnished when dry.

SUITABILITY
Columns, panels, and small objects.

MATERIALS
10% oil-based glaze
10% white spirit/mineral spirits
80% artists' oil paint
Gloss oil-based varnish

EQUIPMENT
Household paintbrush or fitch, for applying glaze
Rag • Hog-hair softening brush
Long-haired sable brush • Varnish brush

POINTS TO CONSIDER
- Try not to make the size or shape of the pebbles too similar, for authenticity they should vary from large and spacious to small and tightly packed.
- The pebble shapes should be irregular and random, do not make them too angular or too rounded.

LEFT *Real breccia marble is often used on large architectural features, as it is not fussy and is patterned with large, pleasing shapes. Therefore it is a good choice of painted decoration for these pilasters in an elegant hallway. It is also fairly quick to paint, making it easier to execute over large surfaces.*

1 Apply the glaze colour very thinly
 and drily, spreading the glaze as far as
possible over the surface.

2 Use a soft rag to wipe angular pebble
 shapes out of the glaze, leaving thin
unwiped areas between. Vary the sizes of
the pebbles, from thin, squashed shapes to
large, open shapes.

3 Soften the whole effect using a softening brush. Because the glaze is so thinly
spread you will probably find it easiest to
use a hog-hair softening brush.

4 When the work is dry, use a long-
 haired sable brush to paint in the veins
(see pp. 80–81). Pay particular attention to
the pebble shapes, encircling them with
angular veins and sometimes veining across
them. Emphasize some parts more strongly
than others, leaving some areas quite plain.

5 Soften the completed effect so that the
 veins do not stand out too much.
Varnish the effect (see pp. 44–45) to give it
an authentic look and feel.

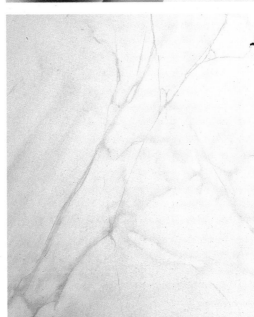

TOP
Raw umber
on white

BOTTOM
Glaze
mixtures of
raw sienna
with blue-
green and
blue with
raw umber
on pale
brown-grey

Specific Marbles

THERE ARE A remarkable variety of marbles in almost every colour and many patterns, from stripy copper-greens to purple manganese spots. Some have dark bases and veins in strong contrast and others are pale, with a cloudy appearance and little veining.

You can paint marble in an authentic way, copying exactly a known marble, or in a decorative way where the patterns of a specific marble are used as initial inspiration only.

Oil-based mediums are the most workable for this technique, but simple marbles can be painted with water-based glazes.

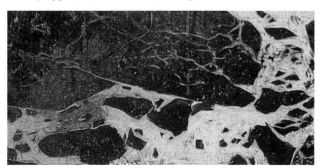

BLACK AND GOLD MARBLE
Black glaze coat. Large veins in yellow ochre and Indian red, and smaller, finer veins in white and yellow ochre. Gold leaf can be used for decorative effect.

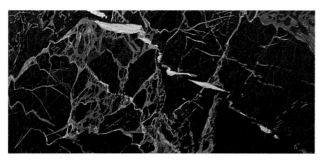

EGYPTIAN GREEN
This uses the same technique as Vert Antique, but with different colours.

GREY MARBLE
White base coat and various grey glazes.

ITALIAN PINK MARBLE
White base coat. Pale, warm terracotta glaze and grey glaze as ground. Vein with the same colours in a deeper tone. Soften and let dry. Vein again with dirtied white.

HOPTON WOOD
This marble is a light, creamy-grey colour, and a sponge is used to create the effect. Cool, pale cream base coat. Light, stone-grey glaze coat mixed with raw umber and white is laid over the base. A sponge is then dipped in the dilutant, squeezed dry, and dabbed over the ground coat. It is then softened lightly with a badger-hair softening brush. Use a flat, square-ended brush to make the stone shapes. Soften then vein in places.

RED DERBYSHIRE
Bright orange-red base coat. Mix glazes using dark red, pale red oxide, and bright yellow in varying degrees of depth and apply over the base to give a mix of dark and light areas. Mutton cloth and soften with a badger-hair softening brush. Distress the ground coat using the method you prefer (see pp. 78–79). Add a little brown-black as your veining colour and soften. Leave to dry. Finally, add dirtied white and grey dots and veins.

SIENNA MARBLE
Off-white base coat. Yellow ochre glaze coat mixed with a little cool brown and white in parts to make three tones. Veined with yellow ochre, brown, and white.

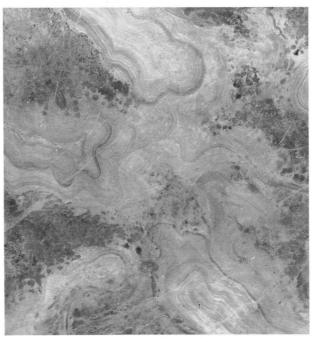

SAINT REMI
Grey base coat. A glaze without colour covers the surface. Burnt sienna and dark red oxide paints are then sponged on in patches. A wide, flat brush is dipped in dilutant and raw sienna paint, with the edges of the brush dipped individually in black and white paint. The brush is then used to make ribbon shapes. Vein with light grey.

WHITE MARBLE
White base coat (perhaps with a subtle drop of blue). Varying tones of grey glaze – grey, green-grey, and yellow-grey – applied and distressed. The veins are painted in deep grey.

VERT ANTIQUE
Worked on a black or deep green base coat. Marble with two or three vibrant green-blue colours and vein in dirtied white.

Malachite

MALACHITE IS COPPER ore, hence the green colour, found in parts of Africa, Chile, America, France, and Russia where some of the most beautiful ornaments and art objects featuring the semi-precious mineral have been made. Malachite was used extravagantly in the great Russian palaces in columns and giant urns. In Italy, it was used as an inlay or sometimes as a tabletop.

The pattern of malachite is made up of incomplete circles, arcs, and spots in deep, rich green and a bright green which varies from grass-green to blue-green. Studying a piece of malachite (try shops and museums) will help to establish the basic formation in your mind. Of all the faux finishes, malachite is probably the one which requires the most thought about its composition.

This technique can be done using water-based materials, but it is more satisfactory to use oil-based products which give greater depth and intensity and allow more time to experiment with the design. You will need to make the malachite markings with a piece of thin, fairly stiff, but flexible cardboard. The thin cardboard used for reinforcing packaging, such as found in some cereal bars, is ideal; cereal packets and other larger boxes tend to be too soft. The size of the cardboard determines the size of the malachite markings, but make sure it is comfortable to hold and move about.

Malachite can look stunning used in combination with other strong, deep colours and rich and complex finishes.

A combination of malachite and gold offers interesting and sumptuous possibilities. You might also like to experiment with the malachite technique using alternative colour combinations to create a completely new, fantasy finish.

SUITABILITY
Small objects, tabletops, panels, and borders.

MATERIALS
Emerald-green base coat
10% oil-based glaze • 5% white spirit/mineral spirits
85% monestial green or phthalocyanine green artists' oil paint
Raw umber artists' oil paint
French ultramarine artists' oil paint
Gloss oil-based varnish

EQUIPMENT
Household paintbrush or fitch, for applying glaze
Mutton cloth • Softening brush
Small pieces of thin, stiff cardboard
Short-haired bristle brush • Varnish brush

POINTS TO CONSIDER
• Make certain the glaze and paint mixture is not too thick. A thick mixture will cause ridges to form when it is marked with the cardboard.

LEFT AND ABOVE *A painted malachite maze on a bathroom wall is an unusual way to use a faux finish which is more often seen on small objects and as inlay on furniture. It was designed and then drawn on the plain white wall in pencil. The areas not to be painted were masked off with tape, and the maze was painted to look like inlaid malachite.*

1 Mix monestial green with a small amount of oil-based glaze and almost no white spirit/mineral spirits. Dab on the glaze, over the emerald green base coat, in random patches, leaving a few areas uncovered.

2 Mix a tiny amount of raw umber into the green glaze, and use it to partially fill the remaining areas. Mix a small amount of French ultramarine into the glaze and fill in the remaining spaces. At this stage the colour variation is very subtle but it will become more apparent in the later stages.

3 Dab a pad of mutton cloth all over the surface quite firmly to eradicate brushmarks and remove excess glaze.

4 Use a softening brush to remove the mutton cloth marks and to achieve a smooth, glossy finish.

5 Fold a piece of thin, flexible cardboard and tear down the fold. The torn edge is the working edge. Describe a circle, applying even pressure to remove glaze colour. Keep one corner of the cardboard roughly in the centre of the circle, to achieve the characteristic malachite shape.

6 Draw another shape that slightly overlaps the first. Continue across the surface.

7 Clean excess paint off the cardboard, or take a fresh piece of cardboard if the first becomes too soggy. Malachite circles vary in size, so use different lengths of cardboard to add authenticity.

8 Twist a short-haired bristle brush in circles to create a few smaller formations of malachite in some of the dark spaces. Take care not to overdo this.

LEFT *A simple wooden box has been exquisitely decorated. It was painted black with malachite inlays. The gold lining (see p. 127) completes a sumptuous colour combination.*

9 Draw a thin line around the malachite shapes by pulling the end of a paintbrush through the glaze in the negative dark areas remaining

10 Soften gently with a softening brush, taking care not to blur the edges of the malachite shapes. Varnish the effect (see pp. 44–45) to give it an authentic look and feel.

TOP
Glaze mixtures of yellow ochre, light red and white, on light yellow

MIDDLE
Glaze mixtures of French ultramarine, burnt umber, and white on bright blue

BOTTOM
Glaze mixtures of French ultramarine, burnt umber, and white on poppy red

11 The overall design is very important; it is helpful to look at a piece of real malachite. Large, complete circles are rare, most are fragmented and split.

RIGHT *Malachite is especially effective on small objects, which it would have been used to make in the past.*

Porphyry

THE WORD PORPHYRY derives from the Greek *porphyrites*, meaning purple, and is used to describe a granular, red-purple rock. The technique of imitating porphyry was introduced to England from Italy in the late 17th century.

The commonest colour for porphyry is a reddish-purple, although there are other varieties. Egyptian porphyry is reddish-orange, brown porphyry veined with quartz and flecked with pink, red, and green is found in Scandinavia, and both green and violet porphyry can be seen in France. The quality and closeness of the texture of porphyry can vary, and it occasionally contains flecks of iron pyrites, known as fool's gold.

To give this technique interest and depth a glaze coat, mixed in a different tone of the base coat colour, needs to be either colourwashed (see pp. 62–63) or mutton clothed, so that the spatter effect does not cover a flat background. The colour of the base and the glaze coats can be pink, red, or orange for an authentic look. For a rich strong colour aim for a bright base with a deeper-toned glaze coat. For a more muted effect mix the glaze in a paler tone of the base colour.

Spattering (see pp. 70–71) with diluted water-based paint in three or more tones of the same basic colours completes the look. Care should be taken to mix the paint to the correct density in order to attain a flat, even surface. If you prefer to use oil-based products then the paint should be thinned with turpentine. Do not mix glaze in the spatter as this causes lumps to form on the surface. You can vary the size of the spattered spots to make the overall spatter effect either fine, or coarse and more granular, by moving the spattering stick nearer to and further away from the painted surface.

The porphyry finish can be translated into any colour, although colours that stay close to the natural feel of the rock probably work best.

Porphyry is used mainly for small, decorative objects like plinths, ornamental bases, and inlays, although larger items have occasionally been made. It has also been much admired as a material for desktops and tabletops. Its density makes it a good finish to use as a contrast with larger types of marble.

SUITABILITY
Bases and inlays, tabletops and columns.

MATERIALS
Glaze • Paint • Gloss varnish

EQUIPMENT
Household paintbrush or fitch, for applying glaze
Mutton cloth • Softening brush (optional)
Fitch or small, short-haired brush, for spattering
Handle of another paintbrush
Varnish brush

POINTS TO CONSIDER
- Test the consistency of the spattering paint frequently.
- Do not add glaze to the spattering paint, this will result in heavy lumps on the surface.
- Don't overload the spattering brush with paint as a little goes a long way.

BELOW *A plain wooden lamp bracket has been given a luxurious and unusual look with a porphyry finish.*

ABOVE *If you find the thought of spattering a large area rather daunting, you can create a similar effect with a sponging-on technique. This column has been given a porphyry finish by applying glaze with a dampened sponge (see pp. 58–59).*

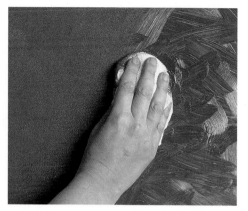

1 Over a red base coat apply a red glaze in a different tone. Mix a lot of paint with the glaze for the strongest colour.

2 Dab a pad of mutton cloth over the surface to provide the depth of finish that will bring the spattering to life.

3 If you think the effect needs toning down you can soften it with a softening brush. Avoid leaving scratch-marks on the surface.

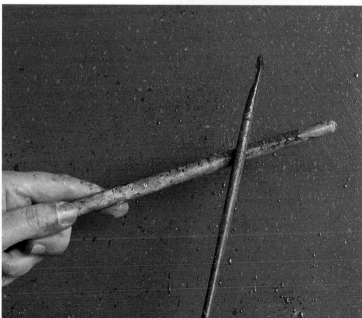

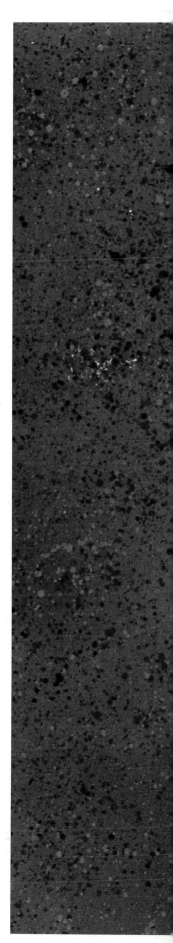

4 Mix three tones of dilute red paint. The paint should be thin enough to run slowly down the side of a container when the brush is wiped on the rim. Load a brush with paint and hit it against the handle of another brush to spatter.

5 Spatter fairly evenly with the three colours all over the surface. Varnish the finished effect (see pp. 44–45) to give the look of stone.

RIGHT Crimson and terracotta glaze with burnt umber and dirty pink spatters, on crimson

Lapis Lazuli

LAPIS LAZULI IS a very attractive blue mineral, speckled with minute crystals of gold-coloured pyrites, called fool's gold. Some lapis lazuli has pale, creamy-grey patches like a drifting Milky Way effect, and some have a tiny amount of veining. It is one of the most valuable opaque ornamental materials, and so is not seen in large quantities. It is often used as inlay on items of furniture or used on small decorative table objects such as boxes and small frames.

In the 15th century, Italian painters ground this stone to produce a sky-blue pigment used for painting the Virgin's mantle in altarpieces. Expensive even then, now it is prohibitive except for use in restoration work. Our modern equivalent is ultramarine.

This stone can be reproduced using water-based materials but, unless you are very skilled, it will be very difficult to achieve the right amount of depth. The recipes given here are for oil-based work. To reproduce lapis lazuli you need to paint both very dark and bright areas of blue with uneven spatters of thinned artists' oil colour and flecks of gold: bronze powder can be used for this (see pp. 144–145). When totally dry it should be varnished and waxed to give it the right look.

The main problem with lapis lazuli is spattering paint of the right consistency so that spots are not raised above the surface in unattractive blobs. Glaze must not be mixed with spattering paint as this causes lumps to form on the surface.

SUITABILITY
Small items of furniture, mainly inlaid.

MATERIALS
10% oil-based glaze • 5% white spirit/mineral spirits
85% artists' oil paint; French ultramarine and burnt umber
3 tones of blue oil-based paint, for spattering
Turpentine, to thin the paint • Bronze powder
Gloss oil-based varnish • Wax

EQUIPMENT
Household paintbrush or fitch, for applying glaze
Mutton cloth • Softening brush
Fitch or small, short-haired paintbrush, for spattering
Handle of another paintbrush
Fitch or small, short-haired paintbrush, for bronze powder
Varnish brush • Fine steel wool • Soft cloth

POINTS TO CONSIDER
- Take care to mix the paint with enough turpentine to spatter the spots evenly without leaving lumps on the surface, but avoid mixing the paint with too much turpentine which will leave 'holes' in the surface of the blue.
- Never spatter with coloured glaze, which will form unattractive lumps on the surface.

1 Mix French ultramarine with glaze, using very little white spirit/mineral spirits. Brush on the central areas of the surface.

2 Paint the remaining areas with a mixture of French ultramarine and burnt umber in the glaze.

3 Dab a pad of mutton cloth over the surface to eradicate brushmarks. The blue should look celestial, clear, and translucent. Lightly brush over the effect with a softening brush. Let the movement of the brush come from your arm, not your wrist.

4 Prepare three tones of oil-based blue paint thinned with turpentine. Load a paintbrush with paint and hit it against the handle of another brush to spatter. Finely spatter the surface in drifts, like the Milky Way.

5 Spatter the lightest tone by pulling back the bristles of the brush with your index finger.

6 Very gently, flick a little gold-coloured bronze powder in drifts to simulate the flecks of fool's gold.

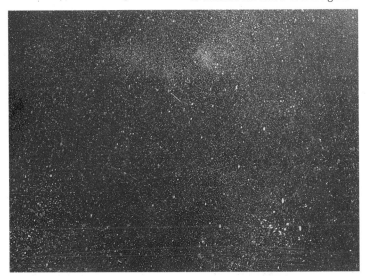

7 Varnish and wax the surface (see pp. 44–45) to give it the look and feel of cold stone.

RIGHT *Lapis lazuli is traditionally combined with precious metals.*

TOP
French ultramarine glaze with pale blue, dark blue, and bronze powder spatters

BOTTOM
Cobalt blue and raw umber glaze mixtures with pale blue and very dark blue spatters

Ribbon Agate

RIBBON AGATE IS a stripy quartz which comes in many different colours. The most common colours are mossy and olive greens as well as yellow ochres. Ribbon agate is often imitated in beige, and sometimes with red that simulates rust marks, but you can also create a more striking and dramatic effect if you use bold colours.

To create the appearance of agate a piece of cardboard large enough to hold in both hands is pulled down the glazed surface – water- or oil-based products can be used – to produce a long, slightly undulating, striped effect. Thin, flexible cardboard used for reinforcing packaging is best. Thick cardboard, such as that used in cereal boxes, tends to become very soggy and makes rather indistinct lines.

Tear the cardboard to form a wide shape that is comfortable to hold and use the torn edge as the working tool. When the cardboard becomes saturated with glaze simply discard it and tear off a new piece.

SUITABILITY
Anything flat, including walls, panels and doors, and furniture such as tables.

MATERIALS
Glaze • Paint • Gloss varnish

EQUIPMENT
Household paintbrush or fitch, for applying glaze
Mutton cloth (optional)
Stiff cardboard • Varnish brush

POINTS TO CONSIDER
• It is difficult to maintain a very long strip over a wall and when you stop to move into a new position the cardboard will leave a horizontal line in the glaze. However, this can easily be incorporated into the overall design.

1 Cover the surface all over with an even layer of the paint and glaze mixture.

2 Add extremely small spots of terracotta glaze to simulate spots where red oxide is naturally found.

3 Dab a pad of mutton cloth over the glaze. When decorating a large surface this step can be omitted.

4 Hold a piece of torn cardboard in both hands and pull the torn end down the surface in a slightly undulating, vertical line.

5 Repeat across the whole surface. Varnish the effect (see pp. 44–45) to give the look and feel of cold stone.

Granite

GRANITE HAS A similar appearance to porphyry and lapis lazuli (see pp. 94–97), but is differently coloured and has a bolder, more robust pattern. The commonest colour is grey, but they can also be brownish-pink, blue-grey, and light greenish-grey. Other colours can be added to blend in with a particular scheme.

You can use a white base coat but using a pastel colour, like pale blue or pale yellow, will give a great deal more depth. The surface of granite ranges from a fine-spotted appearance to a coarser effect. Moving the spattering stick nearer to and farther away from the painted surface will vary the size of the spattered dots (see pp. 70–71) allowing you to control the density of spots.

Granite is not a precious stone, so it is often seen in large expanses and is used in building. It is fairly plain so it looks good used as inlays on a chequered, marbled floor or acting as a foil to something a bit more extravagant.

> ## SUITABILITY
> Floors, columns, ornaments, and borders.
>
> ## MATERIALS
> Glaze • Paint • Gloss varnish
>
> ## EQUIPMENT
> Household paintbrush or fitch,
> for applying glaze
> Mutton cloth • Softening brush • Sponge
> Artist's fitch or small, short-haired
> paintbrush
> Handle of another paintbrush
> Varnish brush
>
> ## POINTS TO CONSIDER
> • Test the consistency of the dilute paint
> before spattering (see pp. 70–71).

1 Paint a grey glaze on the surface. These first two steps can be omitted.

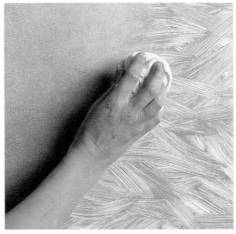

2 Dab a pad of mutton cloth over the glaze to eradicate the brushmarks. Lightly brush over the effect with a softening brush.

3 Use a damp sponge to dab on several tones of grey glaze, starting with the mid-tone and adding darker and lighter tones until you are happy with the general variety and colour.

4 Load a brush with diluted grey paint and hit it against the handle of another paintbrush, to spatter. Spatter evenly using three tones of grey. Varnish (see pp. 44–45) to give the look of stone.

TOP
Brown and
dark brown
on pale
yellow

MIDDLE
Brown with
blue and
white on
white

BOTTOM
Blue with
brown and
white on
pale blue

Tortoiseshell

THE BEAUTIFUL SHIELD-SHAPED back of the Hawksbill sea turtle has long been used for ornamental and decorative objects as it is easily moulded by heat and can be shaped on a lathe. It is more commonly known as tortoiseshell. Apart from its use for jewellery, combs, and boxes tortoiseshell was also used on large pieces of furniture, and when combined with ornamental brass work was referred to as 'boullework', after the creator André Boulle. Sometimes the shell was stained blue, red, or green. Nowadays, using tortoiseshell is illegal in many parts of the world so the desire to paint it is even more intense.

From the 16th century onwards the demand for tortoiseshell outstripped supply, so decorative craftsmen all over Europe were soon using their skills to imitate it. A late 17th-century treatise quotes the imitation of tortoiseshell as much in request for cabinets, tables, and the like. Furniture and mouldings, as well as small objects such as picture and mirror frames, were decorated with the effect and often further embellished with gold. In England and France ceilings, cornices, and woodwork were painted in this manner well into the 19th century.

Tortoiseshell can be imitated using water-based products but it is easier to use oil-based materials which don't dry as quickly, allowing more time to adjust the effect. Because the original tortoiseshell was often stained the imitation can be painted on various coloured bases. However, for the traditional look, the base coat should be white, yellow, or imitation gold leaf for a truly rich effect (see pp. 138–139).

The pattern of tortoiseshell is imitated with a series of strokes and spots of varying widths and lengths painted in a diagonal direction. It varies widely in colour from very dark to very light with an assortment of markings from blotchy, spotty, or stripy to barely patterned. This paint technique is fundamentally different from other techniques. A layer of glaze is applied over the base and then patches of artists' oil paints are added and spattered. Without removing the excess with a rag or mutton cloth, the paint is blended with a softening brush so that the painted spots are spread over the glaze to make smudged spots or streaks.

Real tortoiseshell is used only in small sections and joined together unobtrusively to make a strip or to cover a box for instance. A wall does not have to be painted in the same detail as small-scale tortoiseshell. For an exaggerated fantasy on a wall, the design of the tortoiseshell could be scaled up and a colour omitted to make it easier.

SUITABILITY
Small items, furniture and walls.

MATERIALS
Transfer Dutch metal leaf
Gloss oil-based varnish
50% oil-based glaze • 50% white spirit/mineral spirits
Raw sienna artists' oil paint
Burnt sienna artists' oil paint
Burnt umber artists' oil paint
Turpentine, to thin the paint

EQUIPMENT
Household paintbrush or fitch, for applying glaze
Fitch, for applying oil paints • Softening brush
Fitch or small, short-haired paintbrush, for spattering
Handle of another paintbrush
Sable brush (optional) • Varnish brush

POINTS TO CONSIDER
• Test the consistency of the spattering paint before spattering. It should be thin enough to run slowly down the side of a paint container.

BELOW *Real tortoiseshell was traditionally used on frames, so painted tortoiseshell is especially appropriate here. For effective simulation the frame should not be too elaborate or ornate.*

ABOVE *The tortoiseshell effect was painted over a yellow base on this metal cachepot. Rich, strong colours, such as gold and black, work well as additional decoration.*

1 Brush a mid-yellow glaze mixture over a base of varnished transfer Dutch metal leaf (see pp. 138–139).

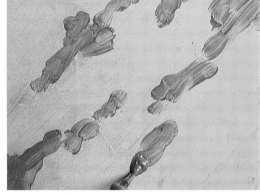

2 Mix raw sienna with a little turpentine so that the paint flows, and brush on in diagonally-pointed cloud shapes. When softened, the colours will merge.

3 Add some small patches of thinned burnt sienna and burnt umber, also working diagonally.

4 Brush over the effect with a softening brush, working in the general direction of the effect so far.

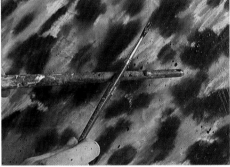

5 Thin some burnt umber with turpentine. Load a brush with paint and hit it against the handle of another brush to spatter.

6 In addition, or as an alternative to spattering, paint small spots of burnt umber with a sable brush.

7 Soften lightly. Adding and softening details over a previously softened area gives a greater feeling of depth.

8 Apply a gloss, oil-based varnish to give a highly-polished look (see pp. 44–45).

TOP
Alizarin crimson and burnt umber on white

BOTTOM
Oxide of chromium and raw umber on white

Moiré

THIS IS RATHER A FUN technique which simulates the wavy, watered look of moire silk. The heartgrainer used for this finish was originally designed for woodgraining techniques. The grainer has a removable head with a series of arch shapes moulded into it and, depending which way the head is placed, will produce either a wide or a narrow grain.

A very thin amount of glaze is applied in strips along a wall. Each strip should be left with an unworked edge into which the next application of glaze can be merged. This action prevents the glaze drying and forming dark stripes. The surface is wiped with a soft cloth to make certain only the barest amount of glaze is left.

A triangular comb and heartgrainer are used alternately, making sure the amount of combing is varied and not too regular. As the heartgrainer is pulled down it is rocked forwards slightly to make the oval heart of the grain. The quicker the rock the more round the heart will be.

The base and glaze colours should be similar in tone but can vary slightly; the pattern of moire is shown by light shining across the watered silk, and too much variance in the tones would look crude. Using subtle colours will produce a delicate-looking, fine finish but more extreme colours can be tried for a more contemporary effect.

SUITABILITY
Walls, panels, and furniture.

MATERIALS
Glaze • Paint • Mid-sheen/satin varnish

EQUIPMENT
Household paintbrush, for applying glaze
Rag • Heartgrainer • Triangular comb
Flogging brush • Varnish brush

POINTS TO CONSIDER
• It is important to use very little glaze mixture for this technique. Too much glaze will smear when the heartgrainer is used.

1 Use a household paintbrush to apply a thin coat of glaze, using an up and down movement.

2 Using a soft rag, wipe a lot of the glaze off, so that only an extremely thin layer remains.

3 Pull down the heartgrainer, gently pivoting it at the same time to make a circular mark. Do this at infrequent intervals.

4 In the spaces between grained strips pull a triangular comb through the glaze to create plain vertical stripes.

5 When the glaze is tacky and nearly dry, drag a flogging brush very lightly down the surface to give a woven appearance.

6 Brush the flogging brush extremely lightly in a horizontal direction to accentuate the look of fabric. Varnish (see pp. 44–45).

RIGHT *This door was given a moiré finish in light blue over dark blue. Moire is always a single colour, but the tones vary slightly. The heartgrainer is unable to go right into corners so panels are usually edged with a hand-painted line next to the moulding, as here. Alternatively you could add braid or wipe glaze away with a cloth or your finger, using the mouldings to keep the lines straight. The panel edges can also be combed or masked off with tape before glazing.*

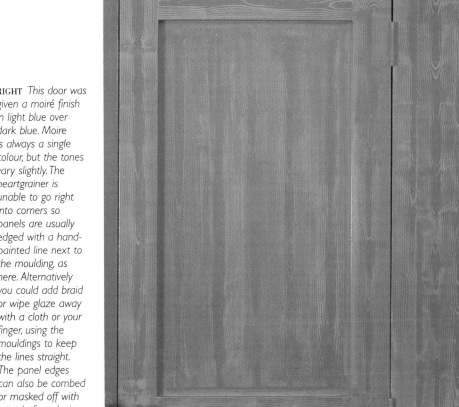

RIGHT
Blue on
sand

Oak

OAK IS ONE OF THE simpler woods to copy, and one of the few that does not require a softening brush. The imitation of oak has been a popular technique for use on woodwork, including doors, panelling, and furniture, since the 18th century.

Natural oak is fairly light in colour and ranges from cream to warm yellow but darkens as it ages. Oak is often limed, making a light, grey-brown colour, or stained in natural tones of dark, warm brown or almost black, or in modern colours like blue and green. All of these effects can be recreated by using varying glaze colours: for a natural oak finish use a pale, warm beige base coat and light, warm grey-brown glaze.

The 'lights' are the angled, broken arch shapes which characterize oak grain. These can be recreated in a variety of ways – using your knuckle, your thumb, a cork wrapped in cloth, or a triangular comb wrapped in cloth.

Oak was often used to panel whole rooms and, if you are going to paint a large area, it is most effective to treat it as panels. They are best drawn in 1-m (3-ft) sheets with a pencil, in the same way as marble panels (see pp. 82–83).

SUITABILITY
Doors, dados, panelling, walls, and most furniture.

MATERIALS
Glaze • Paint
Mid-sheen/satin varnish

EQUIPMENT
Household paintbrush, for applying glaze
Flogging brush
Triangular comb • Graduated comb
Heartgrainer • Cloth • Varnish brush

POINTS TO CONSIDER
- Take care to apply a thin layer of coloured glaze to begin with. If the glaze mixture is applied too thickly the combing will cause unsightly, three-dimensional ridges to form.
- Wood is never the same colour all over so try to vary your glaze colour very slightly with subtle additions of other colours or by adding more of the same colour to make a deeper tone.

1 Choose a base coat colour that is a several tones paler than your glaze. Apply the base coat and allow to dry.

2 Paint on a thin and even coat of glaze with a household paintbrush, using vertical strokes.

3 Drag a flogging brush up and down the surface to thin out the glaze coat.

4 Pull the triangular comb vertically down the surface. Make alternate marks using the triangular and graduated combs.

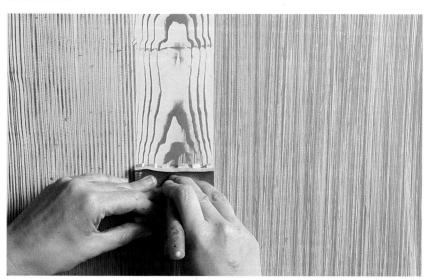

5 Adjust the heartgrainer for painting oak (the wide grain). Pull it down, gently rocking it backwards and forwards as you go.

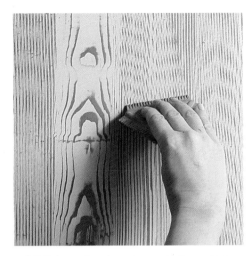

6 Pull down the triangular comb diagonally, to make ticking marks in the vertical grain. Also use the comb over the heart grain to break it up.

7 When the glaze is tacky and nearly dry, hit the surface with the tips of the flogging brush, using a series of upward movements from the ground to the ceiling.

8 Various methods are used to produce the 'lights', such as a thumb or cork wrapped in cloth. Here a triangular comb wrapped in cloth is used to draw the half-arch shapes.

9 Flog the whole effect to give it more texture. Use a mid-sheen/satin varnish to protect the work (see pp. 44–45), and help suggest the feel of real wood.

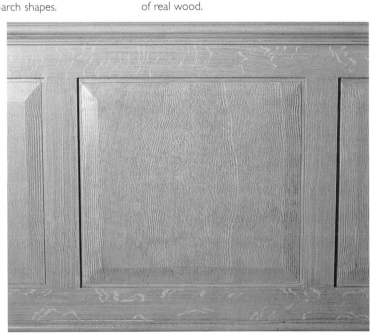

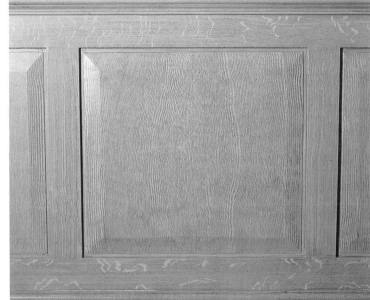

RIGHT *This oak-panelled dado was painted without using a heartgrainer. Instead, various combs were used and lights were added only on the rails.*

TOP
Sienna on white

MIDDLE
Pale blue-grey on sand.

BOTTOM
Raw umber on pale yellow

Bird's-eye Maple

BIRD'S-EYE MAPLE is a pretty wood with a fine, wavy grain and numerous small dots or 'eyes'. It is often used to make picture frames and is an attractive wood to imitate. In colour it is usually a warm, yellow ochre or a cool, reddish-brown. Light browns are also common.

Imitating bird's-eye maple works well when water-based products are used because the technique is similar to watercolour painting. Nevertheless, using oil-based products is also effective, particularly in larger areas where you need the glaze to dry slowly, allowing the area to remain workable for as long as possible.

To achieve the look you need a base coat of white, pink, cream, or yellow. Apply the glaze mixture with a household paintbrush or a mottler by 'wiggling' the brush down the surface, applying more then less pressure to the bristles as you go. To create the eyes, dab your little finger or knuckle into the wettest, darkest areas to lift off the glaze, revealing the base whilst leaving a smaller, darker dot of colour in the centre. Alternatively, you can apply a generous glaze coat, over an area not larger than three widths of the paintbrush, and, with a second brush or mottler, again 'wiggle' in strips down the surface. Then use your finger or knuckle to create the eyes in the same way as before.

The finish can be softened when the glaze is partially dry. This can be difficult and so is an optional step.

SUITABILITY
Small areas, such as panels, and small items such as boxes and frames.

MATERIALS
Glaze • Paint • Mid-sheen/satin varnish

EQUIPMENT
Household paintbrush or mottler
Sponge • Softening brush (optional)
Fine artist's brush (optional) • Varnish brush

POINTS TO CONSIDER
- The glaze mixture should be virtually translucent so use paint sparingly when mixing your colour.
- A small amount of glaze mixture goes a long way, so do not mix it up in large quantities which may never be used.

ABOVE *This panelled dado has been woodgrained in bird's-eye maple using water-based products. Although, over a large area, this method can be difficult to tackle because of the speed with which the glaze dries, it does give a particularly soft and fine effect.*

ABOVE *The bird's-eye maple finish is very effective on this vase holder, since small objects are often made with this wood.*

1 Load a brush with glaze mixture and wiggle it down the surface, varying the pressure on the bristles to make light and dark patches.

2 Dab lightly all over the surface with a damp sponge to break up, but not destroy, the initial grain of the glaze coat.

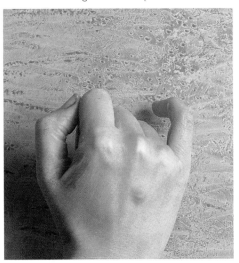

3 While the glaze is still wet, dab either your knuckle or the edge of your little finger into the wettest, darkest areas to make the eyes.

4 The finish can be left to dry and varnished (see pp. 44–45) at this stage, or taken to another stage.

5 When the wettest areas of glaze (the eyes) are nearly dry, brush over the finish in a downward motion using a softening brush.

6 Use a mid-sheen/satin varnish (see pp. 44–45) to protect the work, and help suggest the feel of real wood.

TOP
Light blue
on white

MIDDLE
Orange-red
on white

BOTTOM
Mid-red
on green

Burr Walnut

THIS IS A VERY beautifully-coloured, attractive wood that has, therefore often been painted. Nowadays, it is very expensive and highly prized. In the 1930s there was a fashion for quite dark-stained walnut, but really the best examples are beautiful creamy-yellows. Cutting down the trees and pollarding produce the burrs, clusters of knots twisting and twirling in all directions. Not all walnut is burred; it can be plain but looks rather like a yellow mahogany. Walnut is not usually found in great expanses so quartered panelling is quite frequently done, where four exactly the same veneers are mirrored to make up a pattern. It is a popular wood for flat and panelled doors, both on cupboards and into rooms. It is also a good choice for many items of fine furniture such as desks and tables.

Burr walnut is best imitated using an oil-based glaze, as it is important that the glaze stays wet for a long time, allowing all the manipulation techniques to be carried out. Different tones of brown glaze, from a dark to a warm, light shade, are applied thinly over a pale, cool cream or white base coat. Folded or loosely-held rags are used to wipe over the glaze, twisting and turning to achieve the lines of the grain. Clusters of knots are added by twirling a short-bristled brush into areas which have few grained lines. These can be strengthened too by adding a little paint only and twisting in the same way.

SUITABILITY
Medium-sized and small areas such as door panels, and furniture, such as tables and boxes.

MATERIALS
25% oil-based glaze • 5% white spirit/mineral spirits
70% artists' oil paint; raw umber and raw sienna
Mid-sheen/satin oil-based, varnish
Wax

EQUIPMENT
Household paintbrush, for applying glaze
Soft cloth • Short-bristled paintbrush
Softening brush • Varnish brush • Fine steel wool

POINTS TO CONSIDER
• Take care to apply a fine layer of glaze over the surface so that the base colour can 'shine' through the glaze.

LEFT *The impressive panels of these large doors have been given the burr walnut effect to match real walnut doors in the same hallway.*

ABOVE *A panel was drawn in a satinwood surround and the burr walnut effect only painted within the panel. The moulding, stiles, and rails have been dragged (see pp. 64–66) to give a grained look.*

1 Mix two batches of glaze, one using raw umber and the other with raw sienna. Apply them in random batches over the base coat.

2 Wipe your brush clean before gently brushing back over the surface to blend the two colours together and remove excess glaze.

3 Fold a soft cloth to make a firm edge. Pull the edge of the cloth down the surface, making undulating ribbon shapes.

4 Alternatively, a soft cloth can be crumpled and used to make similar, but less regular, ribbon shapes. Leave spaces between the ribbons.

5 Stipple a short-bristled brush in the areas between the ribbon shapes. Twist the brush to make knots, varying the sizes.

6 Brush a softening brush rigorously in different directions over the entire decorated surface.

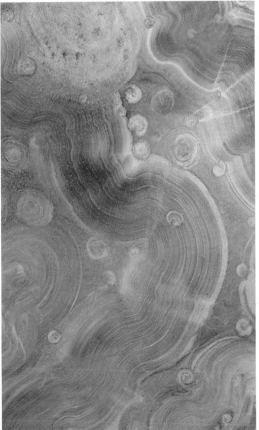

7 Varnish and wax the finished effect (see pp. 44–45) for an authentic look and feel.

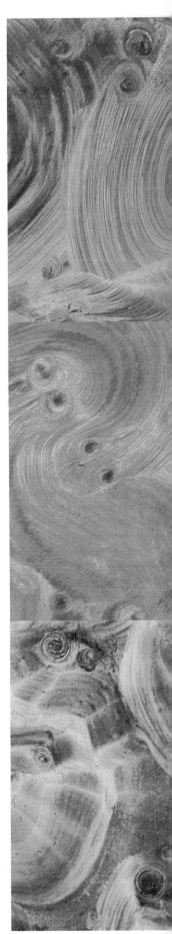

TOP
Raw umber and terra-cotta on grey

MIDDLE
Terracotta and dark brown on white

BOTTOM
Burnt umber and raw sienna on white

Mahogany

MAHOGANY HAS LONG been popular as a fine wood for furniture and doors. The wood is naturally red in colour and is greatly valued for its rich, warm colouring and distinctive and beautiful grain. It has been stained in the past to make it more crimson, orange, or brown.

The pattern of the grain differs according to where in the tree the wood has been taken. There are three different types of pattern. The straight grain is taken from the outer edges of a cross-section; the heart grain from the centre of the cross-section; the feather (also called flame or curl) is cut from the part of the tree where branches grow out of the main trunk, or from the topmost part. The heart grain and feather grain are ideal for door panels, while the straight grain is more suitable for the stiles and rails of a door, skirting-board/base-board, architrave, and dado rail.

Painted mahogany can be extremely effective, and, in some ways, is a good wood for beginners to imitate. The straight grain can be imitated by dragging (see pp. 64–66) and softening across the grain and the feather (illustrated here) is simply achieved once the design and the direction of the brush is understood. Although, as with other woods, there is a tradition of woodgraining with water-based glazes, it is easier for the beginner to work with oil-based products, since they dry slowly.

Mahogany should be painted over a pink or light orange base coat. Warm, terracotta-reds, crimson-reds, and chestnut-browns are needed for the glaze, with a small amount of white spirit/mineral spirits. The glaze mixture should cover but not obliterate the base and there should be an equal quantity over the whole surface. Apply a darker colour to the central area where the feather will be. A dry, flat brush is used to mark the pattern of the grain. This is then softened across the feather in the opposite direction to the flow of the wood.

SUITABILITY
Panels, doors, and large items of furniture.

MATERIALS
20% oil-based glaze • 10% white spirit/mineral spirits
70% artists' oil paint; burnt sienna and alizarin crimson
Burnt umber artists' oil paint • Turpentine, to thin the paint
Mid-sheen/satin oil-based varnish • Wax

EQUIPMENT
Household paintbrush, for applying glaze
Second, dry household paintbrush
Softening brush • Varnish brush
Fine steel wool • Soft cloth

POINTS TO CONSIDER
- If the grain of the wood becomes blurred with the softening then it is likely that there is too much glaze on the surface. Remove a little of the glaze with a cloth or brush and start the graining again.
- Be careful not to be too zealous with the softening brush since over-softening will cause the glaze to break up.

LEFT *These panelled pine doors have been painted in mahogany grain using oil-based products.*

ABOVE *A panelled dado was painted in mahogany grain using water-based products. The stiles and rails have been dragged and then softened in the opposite direction.*

1 Mix a glaze with burnt umber and alizarin crimson and a little white spirit/mineral spirits. Apply to the surface.

2 Mix burnt umber, alizarin crimson, and turpentine and paint in the central area and at the corners of your surface.

3 Wipe the brush clean and brush lightly all over the surface to blend the colours and remove excess glaze.

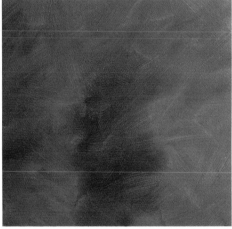

4 At this stage you will have established the basic colour of the mahogany on which the grain can now be marked.

5 Make an arch shape with a dry paintbrush. Keeping the brush at the same angle make more arch shapes, working up the surface.

7 Brush a softening brush across the grain to soften the effect. It may also be necessary to soften with the grain.

6 By building up the arches, leaving no gaps between them, the feather pattern typical of mahogany is imitated.

8 Varnish and wax the finished effect (see pp. 44–45) for an authentic look and feel.

TOP
Raw sienna on sand

MIDDLE
Burnt sienna on pale orange

BOTTOM
Burnt umber on warm, pale brown

CHAPTER V

STENCILLING, STAMPING, AND FREEHAND PAINTING

From potato prints to painted skies, your interpretation of these techniques can be controlled and contained or carefree and exuberant.

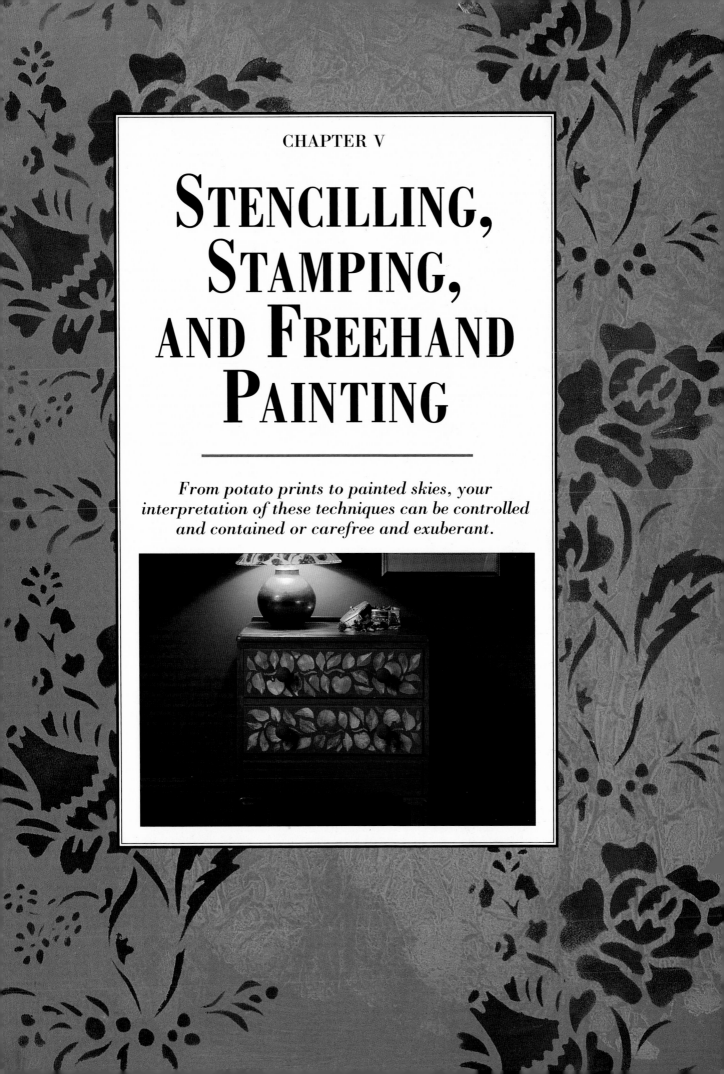

Stencil Sources

THE ART OF STENCILLING is very ancient and has been used as a decorative technique by many cultures. One of the earliest-known English examples is stencilled wallpaper dating from 1509, although the technique was known in the Middle Ages.

Although you can buy ready-cut stencils, designing and cutting your own is far more satisfying. The inspiration for stencil designs can come from many sources, but you should bear in mind the need to keep the shape simple. Natural forms provide a host of ideas; plants, flowers, ferns, leaves, fruit, birds, butterflies, dragonflies, shells, and animals. Museums and stately homes house a wealth of decorative ideas, including woodcarvings, decorated ceramics, screens, garden urns, painted furniture, wrought-iron work, and elaborate picture frames. Needlework, fabric, tapestry designs, and carpets are particularly suitable as they are already two dimensional and separated into the kind of shapes you could easily recreate in a stencil design. Look too at catalogues of exhibitions, illustrated books and magazines, as well as old, second-hand books dealing with ornament and pattern.

LEFT AND ABOVE *A trailing plant was taken as the inspiration for this stencil design. The same stencil has been used in different ways – it has been flipped, turned, and only partly used – to create an arched border which seems not to repeat itself.*

LEFT AND BELOW *This stencil, incorporating two pot plants and a border, was designed for a country kitchen. The designer drew the two plants from life, and added a border to hide marks and splashes from the sink.*

BELOW *Printed sources include Dover books – a pictorial archive series, available from art shops – and second-hand books on architectural ornament.*

RIGHT AND ABOVE *An actual plant can be sketched and simplified to create a unique stencil. Take photographs of flowers or plants that you come across away from home, so that they can then be adapted into stencils.*

Stencilling

THE STENCILLING TECHNIQUE consists of cutting a hole of a certain shape or design into a piece of stencil card or acetate, through which paint can be pushed. It is one of the simplest and easiest ways to decorate a room with a pattern. The results come quickly and the whole process is fairly inexpensive. The great advantage of stencilling is its adaptability. It can fit into the shape and character of a room, whatever its size and dimensions. In addition, a stencil can be used and reused an infinite number of times and in many different ways before it exhausts its impact.

There are many different methods and approaches to stencilling; some people use a very precise method, others have a more flexible and immediate approach. Paints can be applied with a stencil brush, a small roller, or a sponge, or you can use spray paints. The same stencil can be reversed, turned upside down, twisted, and flipped over. It can be repeated, overprinted, used singly, or staggered. The effects and styles possible are endless, from Victorian nostalgia to a strong contemporary look.

The best surface to stencil on is a non-absorbent base, such as a water-based paint with a silk or satin finish, because mistakes can be wiped off with ease using a damp cloth. Some colours, like carmine pinks, may stain and these stubborn paints can be removed with bathroom cleaner. A paint finish protected by varnish also provides a very good surface for stencilling; paint finishes have a 'broken' effect to match the 'broken' effect of the stencil. The varied appearance of an unpainted, plastered wall also looks effective.

Stencils can be bought ready-cut, or they may be ready-printed but still need cutting out. Alternatively you can buy special card or acetate and design your own stencils. Spray the back of the stencil with repositioning glue and leave for a few minutes to set. The stencil will then stick to your surface, even a wall or ceiling, without the use of masking tape or your spare hand.

When applying colours it is very important to use a small amount of paint. Low-vinyl decorative paints or specialist stencil paints should be used. Gently swirl the stencil brush to create a soft look. A stippling movement can also be used, with the brush hitting the surface to make small dots, but this is harder to control.

It is important to work in straight lines along borders and friezes. Even if the floor and ceiling slope, the stencilled border must run straight. At corners you can either use a specially-designed corner stencil or adapt the design you already have.

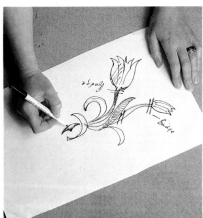

1 Make a rough drawing, indicating where the bridges of the stencil will be. The bridges are the solid strips of card or acetate which hold the stencil together and create the traditional 'broken' look of stencilling. Fill in the areas that you are going to cut out to check that the bridges are in the right places and you are happy with the way the stencil will print.

2 Make a tracing of your drawing, securing the tracing paper to your work surface with masking tape, to prevent it moving. Experienced stencillers sometimes prefer to draw the design directly on to the stencil card.

3 Turn the tracing over and place it over a sheet of stencil card. Scribble over the lines of the tracing with a pencil to transfer the design.

4 Fill in the areas to be cut out. This will help you to concentrate on what you are cutting out, therefore avoiding mistakes.

5 Cut the stencil out using a sharp craft knife. Always pull the knife towards you. When you are cutting around corners, turn the card, not the knife.

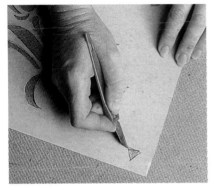

6 If the knife has not cut well and some edges are not sharp, do not worry. This will not be apparent in the finished stencil. Cut any necessary registration marks which will help you line up the stencil on your surface.

7 Test the colours to be used and the stencil on some spare paper before working on the final surface. Use a different brush for each colour with very little paint and add no water to the paint or the brush. Do not completely fill in the holes with colour but leave whiter areas to give depth and shape.

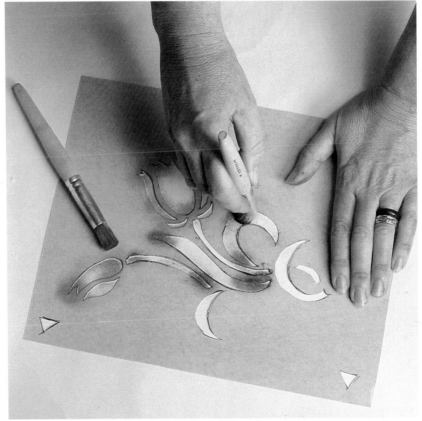

ABOVE *By applying some of the red flower colour to the green leaf areas the design flows, has depth, and looks lively.*

ABOVE *Try out the various ways of using your stencil. You can repeat both the whole stencil and different parts of it. You can also position it at all kinds of angles.*

ABOVE *You can mend a broken stencil with masking tape. Stick a piece of tape over the tear, and stick another piece on the back. Press them into place and recut the stencil.*

ABOVE *When using a particularly large card stencil you will need to secure it with masking tape instead of repositioning glue. A spray repositioning glue will not hold a large piece of card well as it is too heavy.*

ABOVE *This cornice is given interest by the way the stencils are repeated. Although the same border stencil is repeated on each side of the corner, they are not exactly symmetrical, which gives them a unique, natural, and individual feel.*

LEFT *Bows are traditional and popular motifs for stencils because they are flowing and adaptable shapes. Besides being pleasing shapes they also help to make a connecting link between other motifs, giving the stencil continuity and rhythm. Note how the varying intensity of paint gives form to the flowers.*

ABOVE *A classical swag of fruit and leaves has been interpreted in a modern-style stencil. It was painted by using the stencil brush in a wiping motion, with quick-drying artists' oil paint in a mixture of colours.*

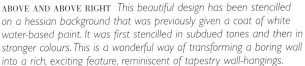

ABOVE AND ABOVE RIGHT *This beautiful design has been stencilled on a hessian background that was previously given a coat of white water-based paint. It was first stencilled in subdued tones and then in stronger colours. This is a wonderful way of transforming a boring wall into a rich, exciting feature, reminiscent of tapestry wall-hangings.*

RIGHT *A window at the bottom of a staircase was stencilled using car spray paints. Three motifs were used and their scale was altered by means of a photocopier; various sizes were tried against the window until the design was satisfactory. Four spray colours were used and allowed to drift on to each motif to give a soft, cloudy look. The spray paints are fairly tough, but the decoration will not withstand a lot of cleaning.*

Stamping

THE TRADITION OF stamping, also known as blocking, lies in the earliest wallpapers of the West and the fabrics of the East and Africa. Paint was applied over a three-dimensional motif carved into blocks of wood and printed on to the surface to make repeating patterns.

You can make your own stamps using a variety of different materials. The easiest and quickest method is to cut a shape out of a close-grained synthetic sponge. The design has to be fairly simple, but you can overprint in different colours to make the result appear more complex. Use the body of the sponge itself as a handle, and, as long as the sponge is washed out after use, it will last for a long time. A fine-grained polystyrene block, like those used in packaging, is also a good material, although it won't last as long as a sponge. Both these materials give a slightly textured print.

You can also cut a design from cardboard and glue it to a wooden block, but a more flexible material is needed when stamping a wall.

To get a good impression the surface needs to be either very flat, or soft and yielding, and when attempting a repeat pattern on a large surface it is advisable to work out a grid first.

You can experiment with different sorts of paint but a thick, densely-coloured, water-based paint is best.

The beauty of stamping lies in the uneven quality of the printed paint, so do not expect perfect results each time the design is printed.

1 Draw a rough outline of your design on a synthetic sponge with a felt-tip pen. Use a sharp knife to cut away the areas of the design that you do not want to print.

2 Either use a brush or a small roller to apply the paint to the sponge. Water-based paints are best but do not use artists' acrylic paints, which dry too quickly.

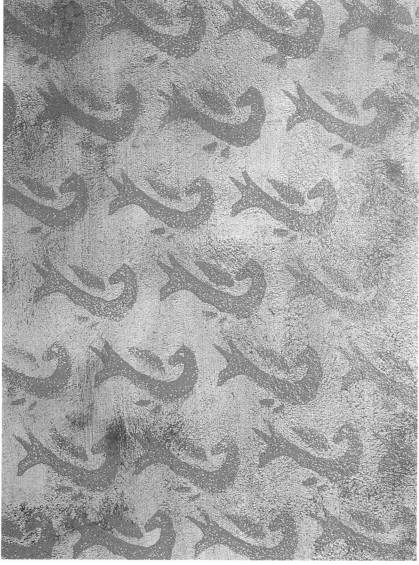

3 Press the stamp firmly, but without too much pressure, on the surface. If you are going to stamp an overall pattern it is advisable to mark occasional guidelines with chalk to help keep the pattern regular. If the pattern starts to print out of line, it is impossible to rectify later and the effect will be unsatisfactory.

1 Draw a design on thick cardboard and cut it out with a sharp knife. Stick the motif on to a wooden block using white wood glue. You can also stick a handle to the other side of the block for ease of use.

2 The paint can be applied to the stamp using a brush or roller before pressing the stamp firmly on the surface. Areas which do not print clearly can be touched in with a brush later.

ABOVE *This design was based on an African motif. It was cut out of a polystyrene block and fixed to a wooden block. The unevenness of paint application is a feature of this technique.*

ABOVE *A flexible sponge stamp will accommodate unevenness in your surface, whereas a hard, block stamp works better on an absolutely flat surface.*

Fruit and Vegetable Stamps

MOST PEOPLE ARE familiar with potato cuts and prints from school-days. It is a simple idea and most kinds of vegetable and fruit can be used with paint to impress a pattern on to a surface. They can be cut horizontally or vertically, used whole, or have patterns cut into them.

Some of the nicest vegetables to use are the most unusual ones; pumpkins, globe artichokes, sweet corn, large swedes/rutabagas, and turnips. Large baking potatoes are very useful and can be used to cut any shape you like. Fruit that has a hard outer skin or firm flesh works best. Apples, pears, oranges, lemons, or even a pomegranate work well. Make sure you can hold your fruit or vegetable stamp securely, or make a handle by sticking a fork into it.

The choice of paint depends on what you have available, but, generally speaking, a thick, water-based paint is best (oil-based paints do not mix with the water in the fruit or vegetables). The paint is simply brushed on to the cut surface before printing. It takes a while for the vegetable to absorb the paint properly and its printing quality will improve with use. Very wet vegetables or fruit are more difficult to use, but eventually the paint will act as a seal and start to permeate the flesh. Try the stamp out on sheets of newspaper first until you get a satisfactory print.

The vegetables cannot be kept, of course, as they soon begin to shrivel, so a design must be completed in one day or a fresh stamp cut for the following day.

ABOVE *A sharp knife should be used to cut a design into a fruit or vegetable stamp. A simple shape, like this chevron, is easy to cut and effective to print. Alternatively, you may find that the vegetable alone has an interesting textured surface, which makes a good print.*

RIGHT *A simple circle of leaves was printed on this door using a potato stamp. The small, blue berries were added by hand.*

ABOVE *A border of chevrons was printed on a frottaged wall (see pp. 52–53) using a potato stamp. The circles were simply printed using a carrot cut in half. Vegetables apply paint unevenly and differently each time, creating a natural, textured effect.*

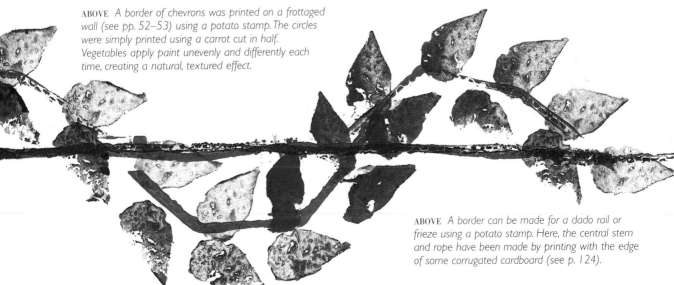

ABOVE *A border can be made for a dado rail or frieze using a potato stamp. Here, the central stem and rope have been made by printing with the edge of some corrugated cardboard (see p. 124).*

Household Stamps

WALLPAPERS USED to be printed by hand and, with some ingenuity and creativity, you can produce something similar at home. The idea is to take a household manufactured object, dip it in paint, and print it on the wall. Suggested objects for this stamping technique include children's wooden blocks, various bottle tops and caps, nail-heads, nuts, bolts, shapes cut out of corrugated cardboard, string, and rope. Alternatively you can mask areas of your surface using masking tape (do not forget you can buy different widths) or masking fluid, which, when removed after painting, will leave the pattern of your choice.

The quality of the print depends on a number of factors; the surface, what you are printing with, and the density of the paint. Absorbent surfaces, such as lining paper, will take a print differently from, say, a non-absorbent, satin wall, and you may want to experiment on a hidden part of your chosen surface before embarking on a complete room. Some absorbent objects need to soak up a certain amount of paint before they will print satisfactorily, so it is also a good idea to test the absorbency of your stamp on some scrap paper before you apply it to the wall. Do not worry if only part of the object prints. Left as it is your motif will look different every time you print it and give a unique variety to your wall. However,

if you are unhappy with the haphazard effect you can always overprint the design, or touch it up later.

Very often objects print differently from the way you expect them to, so you will need to step back and make assessments of the general effect from time to time.

Any paint can be used but a thick, water-based paint which dries to a waterproof finish is the best choice. This way any mistakes can be easily wiped away and brushes are simply washed in water. Artists' acrylic paints can be used, although they tend to be too translucent.

How random or formal you make your design depends on the atmosphere of the room and your patience. A more structured design will need some careful planning using a plumb-line and T-square to ensure that no lines run crookedly.

The essence of this technique is for you to enjoy yourself and to end up with something unusual, creative, and pleasing. Think about colour schemes and coordination carefully before you begin. Simply because this is a light-hearted approach it does not mean your attitude to the preparation should be casual. It is easier to carry it out with panache if you know what you are doing and have thought about it all beforehand. Equally, this does not mean you cannot be adaptable or that you must put yourself in a strait-jacket.

LEFT *A colourwashed wall (see pp. 62–63) was embellished with stamps made from plastic cups and corks from wine bottles. You can develop this idea by adding hand-painted motifs.*

1 Here, the background was colour-washed (see pp. 62–63) and left to dry. Dip the rim of a plastic cup into your paint and use it to print circles. Do not worry if the printing is irregular in places since this is part of the charm of stamping.

2 Dip the cork from a wine bottle into the paint and use this to print solid circles. As you experiment with different objects you will find that some print better than others.

Tree Print Project

THIS MURAL WAS produced almost entirely from stamps made out of swedes/rutabagas and pears. The circle shape of the foliage was roughly painted by hand in dark green and the trunk and pot were frottaged (see pp. 52–53).

When the dark green paint was dry, the leaves were added. These were printed using swedes/rutabagas cut in a variety of leaf shapes. Several thick, water-based paints in shades of green were painted directly on to the swedes/rutabagas and the prints were made in a fairly loose, haphazard manner. The pears were printed using real pears with different colours painted on them before printing. The stalks were added by wiping the wrong end of a paintbrush into the still-wet paint.

Other types of fruit and vegetables could be used. Firm, not-yet-ripe fruit is best since over-ripe fruit leaves a soggy mess.

LEFT *A pear tree was printed on a play-room wall. Other types of trees can also be easily printed using different vegetables and fruit as stamps.*

BELOW *A mixture of greens, ochres, reds, and white was used to build up the foliage and fruit of the tree. Because the fruit and vegetables have a wet texture, they print unevenly.*

Stripes

STRIPES HAVE LONG been an answer to wall decoration, and according to their colour, proportion, and manner, present either a cool and classic look or a contemporary, jazzy feel, with a host of differences in between.

Using any water-based paint, stripes can be produced with straight edges by using masking tape or with soft edges using a roller. Lines with more character can be painted in by hand. A fitch filled with paint and pulled down a wall following a plumb-line or previously drawn chalk line can produce an interesting, wobbly effect.

Stripes can also be made with glaze by dragging or combing (see pp. 64–66 and 68–69).

1 Use masking tape to mark out your stripes over a thoroughly dry base coat. Use a plumb-line to ensure the stripes will be straight.

2 Use the paintbrush to 'feather' the paint over the base coat and overlapping the masking tape. The paint should be quite dry so that it does not run.

3 Fill in some solid stripes, again overlapping the masking tape. Remove the masking tape as soon as your stripes are completed, to reveal perfect straight edges.

LEFT *These dining room walls were decorated in lively, wobbly stripes, painted freehand in three shades of yellow.*

ABOVE *The feathering gives an informal effect, but a more classical look can be achieved by painting solid stripes in traditional colours.*

Lining

INING IS USED as additional decoration on a wide variety of painted furniture. Lines of colour are painted around an area of furniture to sharpen or stress its basic shape, or to provide an extra focus of interest. Although there are various, classic design patterns, the simplest approach is a single line that follows the shape of the surface at the same distance from the edge all the way round. Alternatively, a piece of furniture can also be lined by wiping a lightly-loaded paintbrush along the very edge.

Lining is usually carried out in between the last coat of glaze and the varnishing. Well-finished, professional lining needs a very smooth surface to allow an uninterrupted flow of paint. If the finish is not as smooth as it could be you might apply a coat of varnish and then rub it down with the finest grade of sandpaper to achieve a beautifully smooth surface. Equally, it may be worth finely sanding down the surface with flour paper to eradicate any irregularities in the paint finish.

Swordliners (see p. 29) are excellent for lining, and a brush with longer hairs than an ordinary artists' brush, such as a rigger, is a great alternative for the unpractised.

It is important to make yourself and your hand comfortable. Start lining in a place where your hand gets the longest run with the most control; do not start lining and then find your arm runs out of sweep.

Freehand lining in this way takes a lot of control. You can rest your little finger against the object to keep your hand steady and at an equal distance and height from the surface. The brush must follow the eye and not the other way round; do not watch the brush but look slightly in front of it and trace the line the brush is going to draw with your eye. If you watch your brush, you will certainly wobble.

Be careful not to smudge lines already painted. Work with a small piece of rag to wipe away any unwanted lines. Leave these until they are beginning to dry to get a neat, clean wipe-off without smudges.

ABOVE *These classic dragged hanging shelves (see pp. 64–66) were lined to emphasize their elegant shape. A very dark green paint has been used for the lining with a small arc in the corners giving shape to the rectangle and emphasizing the knobs at the corners.*

1 Load the swordliner with sufficient paint to finish one line at a time. Guide it down the edge of the piece of furniture, keeping your little finger stiff against the edge of the surface. Increasing the pressure will thicken the line, so aim to retain the same pressure throughout.

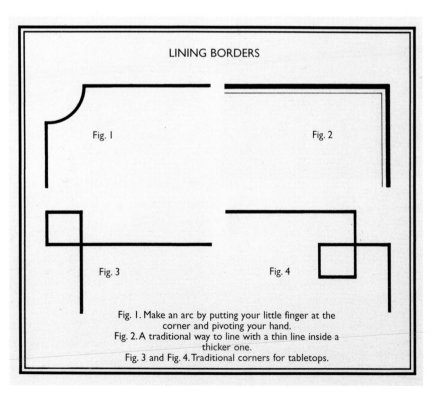

LINING BORDERS

Fig. 1

Fig. 2

Fig. 3

Fig. 4

Fig. 1. Make an arc by putting your little finger at the corner and pivoting your hand.
Fig. 2. A traditional way to line with a thin line inside a thicker one.
Fig. 3 and Fig. 4. Traditional corners for tabletops.

Trompe-l'Oeil

TROMPE-L'OEIL MEANS to deceive or outwit the eye, and this is entirely the purpose of trompe-l'oeil painting. At first sight, a trompe-l'oeil painting must mystify, surprise and beguile the spectator into believing that they are seeing three-dimensional objects rather than a painted, two-dimensional surface. The deception is momentary, since a pause and a second glance are long enough to tell us that we are looking at a painted surface. To be successful the painting has to be more than real, better than a photograph.

The history of trompe-l'oeil begins with an intense desire to paint reality – real objects and people – in the most lifelike way. The discoveries by Renaissance artists of the structure of human anatomy and linear perspective gave them the opportunity to paint with an increasingly virtuoso sense of reality. Along this route to reality artists began to slip jokes into their works, such as life-size paintings of flies on the canvas and pieces of folded paper with signatures on them. Their life-size interpretation often put the picture back into the realm of illusion, while it stood out so fantastically that the folded paper made a regular appearance in trompe-l'oeil paintings.

Later the success with which painters were able to imitate wood led to the use of woodgraining in much trompe-l'oeil painting, either as doors behind open doors, for example, or as tabletops with objects laid down on the horizontal surface. In the 18th century, many fire-screens were being decorated with trompe-l'oeil paintings. They often had an unusual, downward viewpoint.

A simple trompe-l'oeil can be made less arduous by understanding a few basic rules and with the help of good references and a few tips. The first important rule is to keep any objects on the plane of the wall life-size – a coat on a peg, a ticket pinned to the wall, a butterfly on a painted stone wall. Our unconscious visual knowledge is very highly developed, especially where well-known, familiar objects are concerned, and the illusion will not be convincing if an object is reduced or enlarged.

No object should be cut off or incomplete, unlike elements in a conventional painting which may be obscured by the frame. Curtains or architectural stonework like pillars or arches are a convincing way to 'frame' the mural so the picture's illusion is not destroyed at the edges.

Finally, it is necessary to chose a single viewpoint, so that everything will look in correct perspective from that position, and any picture planes in the background, such as a landscape seen through an open window, must have a different light quality and be less clearly defined than the immediate plane.

ABOVE *A painted violin at Chatsworth house, Derbyshire gives passers-by a real trick of the eye. The open door dictates the viewpoint and there is an element of humour.*

1 Position two overlapping playing cards on your surface and draw around them with a coloured pencil. Old cards with creases and character are the most interesting to reproduce. Choose three tones of low-vinyl decorative paint or artists' paints, available from specialist paint shops.

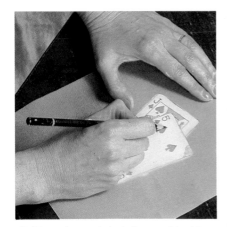

2 Trace the cards, including any blemishes. Turn the tracing paper over and scribble over the pencil marks on some scrap paper. Turn the tracing back the right way up on the table and draw over the outline of the cards to transfer the basic shape.

3 Paint the cards using white artists' acrylic paint.

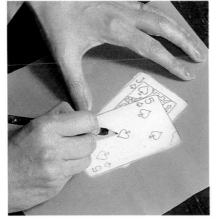

4 When dry, reposition the tracing over the cards and draw over the remaining lines to delineate the separate cards and mark the suits.

5 Start painting with the darkest tone – the black of the spades, the denominations, and the shadows – referring constantly to the actual cards.

6 Add the mid-tone, grey, in areas around the Jack to bring out the difference between the red, blue, and yellow, and in the lighter shadows and creases.

7 Fill in the red, blue, and yellow of the Jack. Paint the lightest of the three tones along the edges, next to the darkest tone, to give sharpness.

8 Mix a thin wash of brown and apply lightly all over the cards. Fill the colour in more densely at the edges and in the creases where dirt would naturally collect.

9 If necessary use the darkest tone to touch up areas where shadows fall. Varnish the entire surface using a mid-sheen/satin varnish (see pp. 44–45).

Trompe-l'Oeil Panels

PAINTING A FLAT SURFACE to make it seem as though it is a three-dimensional panelled shape is an old trick that has been used for hundreds of years. Trompe-l'oeil, meaning trick of the eye, is the technique of painting which is employed to give the illusion of something three dimensional.

Panels can be painted on flat doors and cupboards, walls, or dado areas. The panel can have a large moulding, have bevelled corners and appear to be recessed in, or have raised mouldings. Decide on the style of panelling – extravagant, simple, complex, or restrained – and make preparatory drawings of the whole thing, either full-size or to scale, to anticipate mistakes in measurement, character, or proportion. Try something simple and bold to start.

The direction of the light source must then be decided. The usual convention is to have it coming from above and from the left. This remains consistent even though it might conflict with ceiling lights and some windows.

Realistic trompe-l'oeil panel work is carried out in the colours and finishes which imitate marble or wood (see pp. 74–89 and 104–111), but for a first attempt it is better to work with one colour. This method of monochrome painting is called grisaille work. Although it looks very complex and difficult to do it is merely a question of keeping a clear head and applying logic. Three tones of the one colour are used within the panels – a mid-tone for the inside of the panel itself, a dark tone for the shadows on the left and at the top of the panel, and a light tone for the highlights at the base and the right of the panels. More tones can be used, of course, but the principle remains the same.

Generally, the smaller the room the closer the tones need to be. However, if a painted panel is to be viewed from afar then the tones need to be more exaggerated to be seen.

On a door the painting can be done in flat colour or the door can be dragged.

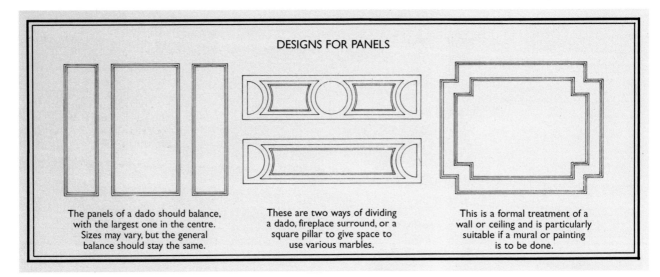

DESIGNS FOR PANELS

The panels of a dado should balance, with the largest one in the centre. Sizes may vary, but the general balance should stay the same.

These are two ways of dividing a dado, fireplace surround, or a square pillar to give space to use various marbles.

This is a formal treatment of a wall or ceiling and is particularly suitable if a mural or painting is to be done.

ABOVE *Panelling does not necessarily have to be painted in a classical manner, but it is important to draw the correct aesthetic proportions to be convincing.*

LEFT *A corridor in Powis Castle was painted to simulate wood panelling. Simply done in just a few tones it works very well.*

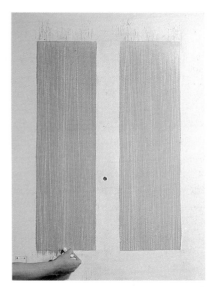

1 Lightly draw your panels on to the door. Mix up two glazes, in different tones of the same colour, and apply the darker tone to the inside of one panel.

2 Use a flogging brush to drag the panel (see p. 67). Glaze and drag the remaining panels one at a time.

3 Wipe the edges of the panels with a soft rag, leaving the stiles and rails clean. You do not have to be too meticulous about this.

4 When the panels are dry, apply the lighter glaze to the rest of the door. Drag with a flogging brush in the appropriate order; centre stiles, rails, outer stiles (see p. 158).

5 As the glaze dries, you may need to apply additional pressure to the bristles with your other hand. This also helps to keep the brush steady.

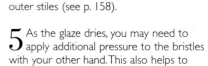

6 Leave to dry overnight. Choose a third and fourth colour, one darker than the panel and one a lot lighter, in low-vinyl decorative paint or artists' paints.

7 Rest a straight-edge against the door at the base of one panel. Apply the lightest colour thickly by pulling the ferrule of the brush along the straight-edge.

8 Then paint the light tone thinly on the right edge. The darkest paint should be applied thickly at the left edge and thinly at the top of the panel. Repeat for each panel.

Stone Blocks

PAINTED STONEWORK has been a popular effect for walls for hundreds of years. In medieval interiors the effect was simply done using just black or red ochre lines to indicate the masonry on an ochre background. Nowadays the effect is generally intended to give some measure of reality.

To give a real trompe-l'oeil illusion, highlights, shadows, and cracks in the stone blocks are painted in, in colours that range from pale, cool, and sandy to warm, yellow, and rich. The most important thing to remember is that the colours should vary on every block. If each block looks exactly the same in colour and tone, the stone wall will look flat and unconvincing. The grouting between the blocks should also

be varied in both width and colour. The grout can be darker or lighter than the stones, but work that will be viewed from a distance will need the strong definition of dark grout lines.

A life-size insect such as a bee or dragonfly, or a key on a hook can be hand-painted in to give interest to the wall.

Here, water-based products have been used and the blocks have been sponged, which is both quick and effective. For a finer and more delicate finish, the blocks could be mutton clothed or stippled (see pp. 48–49 and 54–55).

Stonework is generally done in hallways, entrance halls, stairwells, and cloakrooms but the effect can provide an unobtrusive and restrained background for any room.

1 Very lightly, in pencil, draw a grid of rectangular slabs on the wall. The slabs should be positioned in steps, like bricks. Use a spirit level to ensure your lines are straight. The size of the blocks will depend on the dimensions of the room, but as a general rule, all slabs should be twice as long as their height.

2 Mix glaze and paint in a mid-tone colour of your choice. Here pale ochre is used. Apply the glaze to one slab only, painting all over in all directions. Stipple over the whole slab using a fitch to soften out the brush strokes.

3 Squeeze out a sponge in water so it is sufficiently damp to remove glaze. Dab the sponge on to the glaze to reveal the base coat. Do this in parts of the block remembering to work from the side sometimes and not just on the central area.

4 Mix three slightly darker-toned glazes in a similar colour range. Here a cool brown and a grey have been mixed with a little of the base glaze to make three tones. Dab these on with the same dampened sponge to cover nearly a third of the area.

5 An optional step is to go over the block with a fitch and some of the base colour to give variation. The brush will give a slightly harder mark than the sponge.

6 Repeat Steps 1–5 on alternate slabs. When these slabs are completely dry you can fill in the gaps. For a natural effect you should try to make the slabs vary in colour, tone, and texture, so that some are darker than others, since no stone slab is ever the same.

7 For a more formal effect you can mark your grid out with masking tape, to make the edges perfectly straight. Remove the tape before the decoration has dried.

8 Use a low-vinyl decorative paint or thinned artists' acrylic paint and a fine artist's brush to fill in the grout lines between the slabs. Vary the colour of the grout lines slightly so that they look realistic. You may want to use a long piece of wood or a yardstick to guide you through the straight lines. Make the corners of adjoining slabs look individual and realistic by curving the line or allowing more paint to build up in these areas.

BELOW *A stone block finish is a sophisticated solution for any wall, but is usually applied to hall, staircase, or cloakroom walls. The soft, mellow colours give the effect a feeling of warmth and intimacy.*

Skies

A SKY CAN BE PAINTED on a wall or on a ceiling and is a wonderful way to add space and light to an area. It can also be a backdrop to a trompe-l'oeil painting or combined with a stone wall (see pp. 132–133).

There are, of course, as many different types of sky as there are types of weather and times of the day. The sunlight on the clouds at noon on a summer's day will come from above, while in the late afternoon the light will be from the side. A hint of storm will mean some of the clouds in just one part of the sky scene will be darkened from beneath.

Before beginning, the wall should be prepared with white, non-absorbent paint. It should be smooth without brush strokes so application with a roller is a good idea. Oil-based products have been used in this technique, because they are slow-drying, giving you more time to manipulate and adjust the effect. The use of the stippling brush helps to give depth to the colours and evens out the gradual changes in tone.

The following is a guide to a systematic approach to painting a sky, that can be adapted to suit your needs. The size, shape, and number of clouds can be changed and the blue can be deeper or lighter depending on the type of room it is in. This sky scene is painted on a wall and so uses an arch-shape structure. For a ceiling, it is necessary to make an oval or a circle to achieve the correct spatial feeling.

1 Mix seven glazes in graduating tones of blue. Apply the lightest blue glaze over a white base coat. Brush it on horizontally then even it out by brushing over it vertically and horizontally. Apply the darkest glaze colour in a sweeping arc at the top of the surface.

2 Working down the surface, apply another five arcs of glaze colour, graduating from the darkest at the top to the lightest at the bottom. Stand back from your work often and fill in areas of glaze where needed.

3 Soften the whole effect by firmly dabbing the surface with a large stippling brush, working upward. You will need to work quite quickly to soften the whole effect before the glaze dries.

4 To make a cloud, pinch a small section of cotton rag between your fingers. Rub the rag into the glaze in a small, swirling motion, removing the glaze and creating a series of semicircular shapes. Rub over the shapes with the rag a second time to soften the effect.

5 Soften the whole cloud using a stippling brush. Repeat to make more clouds, an odd number looks best. Stand back from your work often to judge the overall effect. Use the rag to rub a few thin lines of cloud towards the bottom of your surface, and soften them with a stippling brush.

6 Fill in the area from the top of the surface to the highest clouds, and around their edges, by applying sweeping strokes of the darkest glaze colour. Use the stippling brush again to soften the effect.

7 To achieve the look of sunlight coming in from the top left of your wall, pinch a piece of rag between your thumb and forefinger. Rub the rag back into the clouds, highlighting the arcs.

LEFT *The puffy white clouds scudding across the clear, cobalt-blue sky on this wall are reminiscent of a summers day. The clouds are varied in size and quite compact, except for those at the bottom, which are long and thin.*

BELOW *The unusual shape of the ceiling inspired this sky painting. The feeling of depth is created by applying ovals of colour with the darkest at the outside edges and the lightest and brightest in the centre.*

CHAPTER VI

GILDING
AND
ANTIQUING

Use these techniques on their own or as a final embellishment to add contemporary sparkle, traditional splendour, or patinas that conjure up the past.

Simple Gilding

WHERE TRADITIONAL gilding uses very delicate, real gold leaf, a simpler method for the novice uses imitation gold leaf called Dutch metal – as well as copper, silver, or aluminium leaf – adhered to a surface with either water- or oil-based gold size. Metal leaf is sold in loose and transfer forms. The transfer metal leaf is more expensive, but is backed with waxed paper, making it easier to handle.

Water-based size is white in colour when wet. It is applied to the surface and after several minutes – the time depends on the absorbency of the surface – the size is quite transparent. The surface is now ready to be gilded and will be slightly sticky to the touch. Water-based size remains tacky indefinitely and can be gilded at any time.

Oil-based size is a traditional product which remains tacky for only a short time. Its drying time depends on the product and type of surface it is applied to, but it eventually becomes unworkable. Use oil-based size if you do not want to cover the whole sized surface with metal leaf.

The application of size darkens an absorbent base, making it easy to see where to gild. When applied to a non-absorbent surface, however, it is not so apparent. To make it obvious, colour the size with pigment or buy ready-coloured size.

LEFT *Dutch metal leaf was applied to this chair, leaving just part of the legs unadorned. The decoration complements the stencilled wall in the background which has been embellished with metal leaf on just some of the leaves.*

1 Use a paintbrush to apply a coat of water-based size to the surface. Water-based size remains tacky indefinitely, which makes it a good medium for the beginner to use.

2 Position the transfer metal leaf, holding it by the overhanging waxed paper. Slightly overlap the edges of adjacent sheets.

3 Smooth over the waxed paper with your fingers, particularly at the edges. As the transfer metal leaf adheres to the size the waxed paper will come loose.

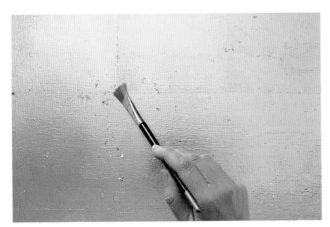

4 Gently wipe excess metal leaf from the overlapping sheets using a soft brush. Reapply pieces of metal leaf to any gaps, using more pressure. Any areas which have been covered with water-based size but not gilded should be varnished, waxed (see pp. 44–45), or dusted lightly with talcum powder.

LEFT AND ABOVE *Transfer metal leaf can be cut with scissors. Transfer Dutch metal leaf was cut into thin strips, and applied to parts of the turned chair leg. The shiny metal is in direct contrast to the muted creamy-brown of the visible leg.*

1 To gild an accurate thin line, first use masking tape to mask off the area that you do not want to gild.

2 Paint a thin layer of size, here oil-based size, in the masked off line. Using masking tape as a guideline means you do not need to be too accurate with the size.

3 Use scissors to cut a strip of transfer metal leaf and position it over the sized surface. Smooth over the waxed backing paper with cotton wool.

4 Carefully remove the backing paper. If, when you lift the waxed paper, you find that the leaf has not adhered properly, smooth it back down and apply more pressure with your fingertips.

5 When the whole surface is complete, carefully lift the masking tape, to reveal a thin, straight line of gilded decoration.

Gesso

GESSO CREATES AN extremely smooth and porous surface which is very useful as a base for many decorative techniques, especially traditional gilding. Gesso has a long history in furniture and frame decoration and the recipe that is used today is probably the same as that used by the ancient Egyptians.

Gesso is a white liquid which is made from a fine white chalk, known as whiting, mixed with warmed liquid size or glue made from rabbit skin. Rabbit-skin glue is available in granules and sheets from most art shops.

Gesso has several characteristics. It can be drawn into with combs and pressed with punches to make three-dimensional designs, and, when it is completely dry, it can also be carved. Its smooth, porous surface allows paint or size to be absorbed without soaking in completely.

Gesso is essential as a base for traditional gilding methods. It is the only surface smooth enough to take the wafer-thin leaves of gold without tearing them, allowing the gold to be safely burnished to a high shine. Several layers of gesso must be built up to create the smooth surface, as many as five to eight coats is usual.

Gesso is quite easy to prepare, but time consuming. The rabbit-skin glue granules are soaked in water and melted down to make the size. On cooling the size solidifies into a gel and can be liquefied again by reheating over a double boiler. Once made up, however, the size has a limited life. Excess can be stored in the refrigerator, but it tends to thicken, and diluting it with water is unsatisfactory as it makes a weaker solution. It is best to make fresh mixtures as you need them.

Generally, whiting is added to the size until it has absorbed all the liquid. When the mixture is stirred, it becomes liquid again. The greater your skill, the more whiting you can add to control the thickness of your gesso. A thicker mixture has the advantage of drying quickly, but is more prone to air bubbles which disturb the smooth surface.

To use gesso you simply brush it on to a surface and build it up in layers. Each layer should be lightly sanded before the next layer is applied.

Gesso is quite often coloured with a layer of bole before the gold leaf is laid on. Bole is a soft liquid clay which is mixed with rabbit-skin glue. It is usually red oxide in colour but can also be found in white and yellow ochre. Red is the colour traditionally used for gilding because it contrasts beautifully with the gold, and this decoration is often seen on frames. Yellow as a base is more usual on ceilings and cornices where total coverage in leaf is not essential since close inspection is not possible. A white base is more commonly used on furniture where a lighter effect is needed.

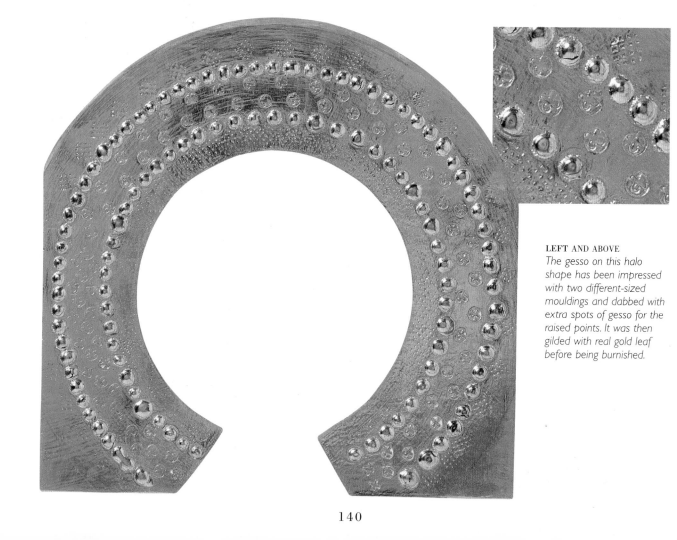

LEFT AND ABOVE
The gesso on this halo shape has been impressed with two different-sized mouldings and dabbed with extra spots of gesso for the raised points. It was then gilded with real gold leaf before being burnished.

1 Using a ratio of one part rabbit-skin glue granules to ten parts cold water, soak the granules overnight.

2 The next day, add another ten parts water. Position the bowl containing the mixture in a saucepan of hot water and stir until the granules have completely dissolved. Alternatively you can heat the mixture in a double burner.

3 Add whiting to the melted granules in small amounts until the whiting has absorbed all the liquid. Stir the mixture until it reverts to liquid form.

4 Stretch some clean nylon mesh (such as an old pair of tights/pantyhose) over a clean bowl and gently pour the liquid into the sieve. Leave the liquid to drip through the mesh. You can store any excess gesso in a refrigerator, but it does tend to thicken.

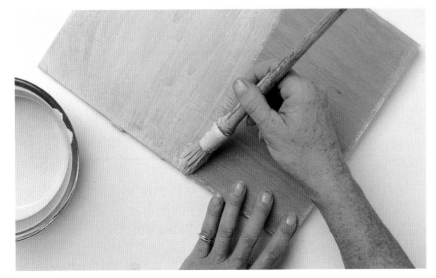

5 Sand the surface you are going to cover. Paint a thin layer of gesso on to the surface, brushing in one direction only to produce a smooth, even layer. Leave to dry and sand lightly before applying subsequent layers.

6 Apply a thin second layer, this time working the brush in the opposite direction. Apply a minimum of five coats, sanding lightly between applications.

Traditional Gilding

THIS TECHNIQUE REQUIRES a lot of practice to perfect, and is therefore not recommended for complete beginners. The traditional method uses real gold in loose-leaf form and a water-based size made from rabbit-skin glue granules, water, and methylated spirits. The leaf is very light and is easily disturbed by the slightest draught. It must be prepared on a traditional gilder's pad which has a static-free parchment surround to protect the leaf. The leaf is handled by either lightly greasing or building up static electricity on a wide but delicate brush called a gilder's tip. The natural oils in the hair or skin can be enough to pick the leaf up.

The size is applied to a gessoed surface (see pp. 140–141) and the gold put on speedily as the size dries quickly. The leaf is then burnished to a high shine with an agate-tipped tool.

1 Dilute some rabbit-skin glue size (see p. 141 Steps 1–2) with water and a tiny drop of methylated spirits until you have a watery mixture. Real gold leaf should not be touched with hands, so transfer it gently to a gilder's pad. The parchment wall protects the leaf from draughts.

2 Gently tease the gold leaf with the flat side of a gilder's knife to adjust it to lie flat. Keep all your tools in one hand to minimize the amount of movement.

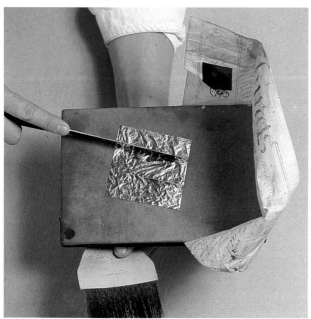

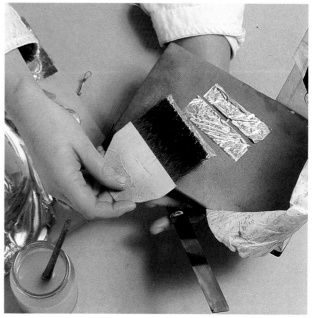

3 Cut the gold leaf to the appropriate size with the gilder's knife. Work close to the object you are going to gild to minimize disturbance to the gold leaf.

4 Very gently lift the gold leaf using the gilder's tip. If, at first, the tip will not pick up the leaf, brush it against your cheek to gather a little natural grease from the skin which should then pick up the gold leaf from the pad.

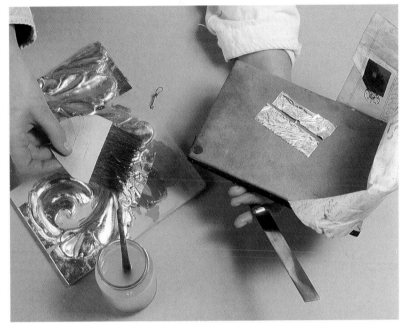

5 Make sure the surface you are gilding is completely dust free. Hold the tip with the gold leaf in one hand and paint the area to be gilded with your size, water, and methylated spirits mixture.

6 With the tip, gently place the gold leaf in position while the size mixture is still wet. It cannot be adjusted once it has been laid down.

BELOW *The high polish and perfection of gilding sometimes looks ostentatious. This frame has been gilded over red bole and distressed with a mixture of white spirit/mineral spirits, wax, and pigment washed over it and rubbed into it with steel wool.*

7 As the size mixture dries the gold leaf will adhere. You can help the leaf to adhere by gently pushing it, not stroking it, with cotton wool. When you have gilded the whole surface leave to dry thoroughly.

8 When completely dry, burnish the gold leaf to a high shine. You can be quite vigorous about this and, provided there is no dust or grit under the surface, it will not tear. The smooth gesso background also ensures that the leaf does not tear.

Bronze Powders and Metallic Wax

BRONZE POWDERS, DESPITE their name, are actually made from various metals, including copper and zinc. They are extremely fine powders available in approximately twelve metallic colours from silver, through the various gold colours, to copper. Bronze powders produce less shine than metal leaf, but they are generally easier and cheaper to use.

Bronze powders can be used in several ways. The traditional method is to apply gold size to a design, and then brush the bronze powders gently on to the size. This method was used to decorate 18th- and 19th-century lacquerware in Europe and folk work in America. It was a style created to imitate earlier Chinese decoration and was often carried out over black bases and occasionally on dark red or green bases. Chairs, small tables, trays, and boxes were popular items for this treatment.

Bronze powders can also be used to colour clear or neutral wax by mixing enough powder to produce a solid colour. The coloured metallic wax is applied with the finger over carved items and mouldings and can even be used to stencil designs over a matt paint (see pp. 114–119). Metallic waxes can also be bought ready-made.

Bronze powders are very fine and likely to be blown away by the slightest draught and if you plan to use them frequently it is a good idea to wear a face mask.

Bronze powders will tarnish with time and therefore should be protected with varnish (see pp. 44–45).

1 Paint a design on the surface in water-based gold size – you may decide to trace a design or draw it on lightly in pencil first.

2 When the size has dried a little and is tacky, take a small amount of bronze powder on a bristle brush. Brush the powder on to the drawing, pushing it ahead of the brush to minimize the chance of smudging.

3 Leave areas of the design unpowdered and fill them in with different-coloured bronze powders.

4 When the design is completely covered, use a soft bristle brush to dust away the loose powder, revealing the design. Excess powder can be collected and used again. Varnish the final effect (see pp. 44–45) to stop the powders tarnishing.

1 To make a metallic wax, take some clear or neutral wax and add to it approximately the same amount of bronze powder. Don't worry if you make too much because any surplus can be stored in an airtight container.

2 Use a palette knife, or other pliable knife, to mix the wax and bronze powders until they are completely blended and no streaks remain. It is easiest to mix them in a small dish.

3 Apply the metallic wax by spreading it over the surface with your fingertip. Always apply the wax in one direction. You can choose to cover a surface densely or, to create an uneven texture, wipe the wax gently on so that areas of the paint below show through.

BELOW *Two tones of metallic wax, a warm, reddish-gold and a light, yellowish-gold, have been used to highlight the tips of the carvings on this blue-stained, wooden frame.*

ABOVE *This beautiful primrose was produced by brushing bronze powders on to a design painted in oil-based size. The density of powder varies for a lively effect. The veining and flower centres were added using paint.*

Crackle Varnish

THIS AGEING TECHNIQUE uses a two-part medium to imitate craquelure, a network of fine cracks in a painting or its varnish. Think of the look of varnish on an old master painting that has cracked as it ages. The cracks have filled with dirt over the years producing a series of fine lines. In decorating this technique is usually applied to furniture.

The cracks are formed by applying one varnish on top of another. The different drying times of the varnishes causes the two layers to react with one another, making the top layer crack. There are several two-part kits available. Some contain an oil-based varnish for the first layer and a water-based varnish for the top coat, while others consist of two water-based varnishes.

Crackle varnish should not be applied to a surface that is very absorbent; the first varnish will sink into the surface, leaving nothing for the top coat to react with. It is also important to judge carefully when to apply the top layer. If the first layer is too dry there will be few or no cracks, if too wet the top coat will not adhere. With practice you will be able to control the size of the cracks since a thick coat of the first varnish will produce larger cracks than a thin coat.

Crackle varnish can be applied over any decoration, such as a plain background, stencilling, hand painting, gilding, or one of the glazed paint finishes. For the cracks to really stand out you should work with a pale base and colour the cracks with dark artists' oil paint. You can also achieve interesting results by using crackle varnish over dark backgrounds such as rich, dark red, blue, or green. Highlight the cracks with a lighter colour – but not white – or gold metallic wax.

1 Apply a thin coat of the first varnish to a clean, smooth, not too absorbent surface. The thicker the varnish coat the larger the cracks will be and the longer it will take to dry. Wait for the varnish to become nearly dry.

2 When your finger does not stick as you run it lightly across the surface, but does adhere when you press it down on the surface, apply a thin coat of the second varnish. The surface will reject the varnish if the the first layer is too wet.

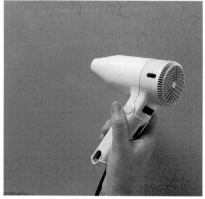

3 Allow the surface to dry in a warm atmosphere which will encourage the cracks to develop. To speed the process you can use a hair-drier, but do not over-heat as this causes the top layer to peel off.

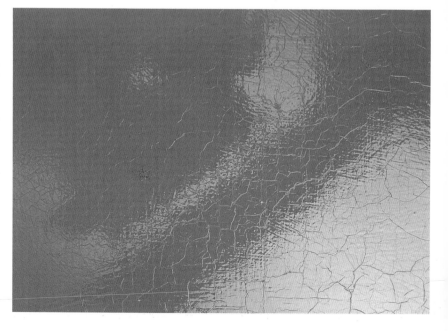

4 When the surface is completely dry, which can take up to six hours, rub a dark artists' oil paint into the surface with a cotton rag. Use a circular motion to push the paint into the cracks.

5 While the artists' oil paint is still wet, wipe away the excess with a clean cotton rag so that the paint only remains in the cracks. Cover with a final coat of oil-based varnish for protection (see pp. 44–45).

BELOW *A paper border at the top of a wall was varnished to make the paper less absorbent. The uneven look of natural age-ing was achieved by only applying the second varnish coat in random areas, resulting in dark patches where artists' oil paint has settled in the cracks.*

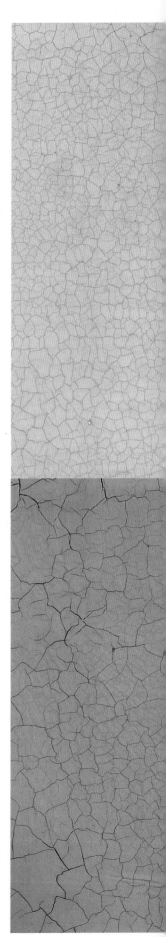

TOP
Crimson artists' oil paint on pale yellow

BOTTOM
Blue-green artists' oil paint on pale yellow

Crackleglaze

THE USE OF CRACKLEGLAZE, also known as peeling paint medium or cracking compound, imitates the look of paint that has cracked with age, allowing the colour beneath to be seen through the cracks.

A layer of crackleglaze is sandwiched between two, different-coloured, water-based paints and causes the top layer to crack. Use low-vinyl paints if you can, but matt emulsion/ flat latex paints will also work. There are many commercial brands of crackleglaze available, all based on the same principle, but each reacting in slightly different ways.

This technique works best on a surface that is not too absorbent. To seal an absorbent surface apply a few coats of water-based paint or varnish.

Take care not to overbrush the final coat of paint, which may cause the crackleglaze medium to coagulate, making a lumpy mess. Instead you should brush once or twice in the same area, rather than repeatedly. The direction of brush strokes dictates the direction the cracks will take, so use your brush in lots of different ways. The cracks appear after approximately one minute. Leave the work to dry undisturbed, as the surface is quite fragile until it is completely dry.

This effect needs to be protected, because it will begin to flake off, although possibly not for several years. Protect with wax or a patinating medium (see p. 152) or coat with oil-based varnish (see pp. 44–45). Do not varnish with a water-based varnish, as this will begin to crack too.

1 Apply a coat of water-based paint to a surface that is not too absorbent. You may want to apply two or three coats of paint or a water-based varnish to seal the surface.

2 Apply an even coat of crackleglaze medium to the surface. The thicker the coat the larger the cracks will be. Allow the crackleglaze to dry for at least four hours.

3 Apply a coat of water-based paint in a different colour. Do not overbrush. The direction you brush in dictates the direction the cracks will take. Here, we have brushed in all directions using short brush strokes. Use oil-based varnish or wax to protect the effect (see pp. 44–45).

OPPOSITE *Inspired by old and cracked pottery in the country style, a wooden salad bowl was decorated using crackleglaze medium between a terracotta base paint and an off-white top coat. The cracks were emphasized by using a dark wax.*

RIGHT *The crackleglaze on this terracotta pot was sandwiched between a dark blue base coat and a yellow ochre top coat. The finish was protected with a coat of clear wax.*

TOP
Grey-blue on
yellow ochre

MIDDLE
Yellow ochre
on dark
yellow

BOTTOM
Peach on
black

Colouring and Distressing Varnish

YOU CAN GIVE YOUR work an aged effect and protect it at the same time by colouring a coat of water-based varnish. Water-based varnish can also be scratched with steel wool for a time-worn look.

To colour varnish sprinkle powder pigment on to an even layer of still-wet varnish. Choose a pigment which dulls and complements the colour beneath. Take care with the strength of pigments, however, as they vary from very weak to extremely strong, so try only a small amount at a time. To vary the effect use two or three pigments of the same general tone.

You can give varnish a distressed look by scratching it with coarse steel wool once it has dried and emphasizing the scratches with dark paint. The varnish must be completely dry before you scratch it, otherwise it will just peel off, and the paint must be water-based – a low-vinyl paint available from specialist paint suppliers is best. Generally all excess paint is wiped away from the surface leaving colours only in the scratches, but touches of colour can be left on the surface if you prefer. A final coat of varnish is necessary to seal and protect the effect (see pp. 44–45).

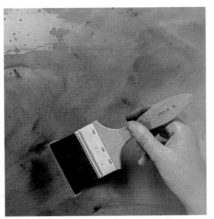

1 Sprinkle a small amount of pigment on to a layer of still-wet water-based varnish. Rub the pigment between your fingers first to get rid of any lumps.

2 Brush the pigment out and into the varnish. Try to brush out any spots that are too large, but keep the effect varied.

1 Apply a coat of water-based varnish to your surface and leave to dry thoroughly. Use very coarse steel wool to scratch into the surface, scratching in all directions, using both long and short strokes. Avoid using circular motions which look unnatural.

2 Use a firm-bristled brush to work water-based paint into the scratchmarks. A specialist low-vinyl paint is best. Use as many colours as you like but keep to dark-coloured paints for an authentic, aged effect.

3 While the paint is still wet wipe over the surface with a damp sponge to remove the excess paint so that colour only remains in the scratchmarks. When the paint is dry apply a final coat of varnish to protect and seal the effect (see pp. 44–45).

OPPOSITE *The stencilled chair (see pp. 114–119) was varnished several times before being scratched with steel wool. Paints in terracotta, green, and a little blue were used to accentuate the scratchmarks.*

Distressing with Wax

To GIVE THE IMPRESSION that a layer of paint on a surface has worn away in places, wax is used. It softens water-based paint, making it easier to rub back with steel wool. Wax contains a white spirit/mineral spirits solvent that is drawn into the surface. Patinating medium, a similar material, works in the same way but is purely water bound.

Wax must be applied to an absorbent surface. When distressing paint with wax it is best to do so with matt, low-vinyl base paint, which is available in specialist paint shops. Shiny surfaces, such as gloss paint, are not suitable because they have shields that prevent the wax penetrating.

If you apply a coat of paint and wax to a wood base, when you rub it back with steel wool the wood will be revealed. If the wood is new it will look rather bright so this effect is better used over old wood. Alternatively, you can apply two or more paint colours on top of one another, and rub the top coat back with varying degrees of force so that in some places the paint underneath is revealed and in other areas the paint is rubbed back right to the wood. By choosing fine or coarse steel wool, the paint can be rubbed gently or firmly to control the amount of paint that is removed.

Typical base colours for this technique are traditional shades of terracotta, grey, and off-white.

To look authentic, it is a good idea to distress with wax in those areas which naturally get the most wear, such as near the handles on a door and the edges of a table.

LEFT *This cupboard was painted deep terracotta then dark green, with a grey diamond stencilled over the top (see pp. 114–119). Dark wax was used to soften the paint which was rubbed back to reveal the terracotta base paint, and, in places, the wood. Special attention was given to those areas which would naturally get a lot of use, the handle, keyhole, and some edges.*

1 Use fine steel wool to spread a layer of wax over a dry coat of matt water-based paint. You can use clear or dark wax. Rub the wax in gently so that the paint absorbs it.

2 While the wax is still wet, rub hard in one direction with coarse steel wool, revealing the layer beneath the paint.

3 You can use fine steel wool to produce a more subtle effect. The fine steel wool will remove less paint.

4 Apply another layer of wax over the surface, using fine steel wool. This layer serves to protect the areas where wax was removed by the distressing technique.

5 Allow the wax to dry for approximately twenty minutes. Use a soft cotton rag to buff the surface to a soft sheen.

TOP
Forest green on ultra-marine blue

MIDDLE
Off-white on yellow ochre

BOTTOM
Light grey on Bordeaux red

CHAPTER VII

THE REST OF THE ROOM

The doors, windows, fireplaces, furniture, and the rest of the room should complement the decoration on the walls. The following examples will inspire and inform you of some of the best ways to bring focus and interest to your rooms.

Panels and Kitchen Units

PANELS CAN BE TREATED in many different ways. The centre of a panel provides a platform for basic finishes, such as ragging, sponging, or combing (see pp. 50–51, 58–61, and 68–69), while the rails and stiles should be kept plain, or simply dragged, flogged, or wiped with a cloth (see pp. 64–67). Raised, ornate mouldings are best wiped.

To provide focus a panel can be treated like a picture frame, with a freehand design or stencilled motif painted within (see pp. 114–119). False panels can be painted on to a plain cupboard using trompe-l'oeil techniques (see pp. 130–131).

If cupboard panels in a room are to provide the focus of attention it is a good idea to keep the colours and finish of the walls simple, so that they complement each other, rather than competing for attention.

Kitchen units also offer plenty of possibilities. Wood can be painted easily, but if it is already painted or varnished it will need to be either rubbed down, stripped, or painted with a low-vinyl paint to provide a good key. Melamine, the plastic-like material which many kitchen units are made of, can be painted with a low-vinyl paint before decorating. Varnish them well to protect against the heavy wear they inevitably suffer (see pp. 44–45). The surface of white goods, such as fridges and dishwashers, can be stencilled directly, although the decoration will wear after about three years without varnish.

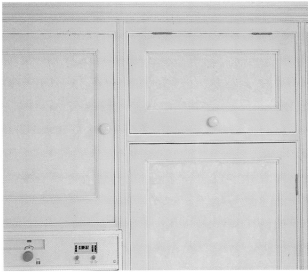

ABOVE *This whole kitchen has been stippled in yellow ochre. Texture is provided by the rag-rolled panels and wiped mouldings (see pp. 54–57).*

LEFT *A freehand painting in artists' acrylic paints can enliven a conventional, laminated kitchen unit.*

OPPOSITE *Spray paint adheres well to shiny, impervious surfaces, and was used here with a number of stencils.*

BELOW *A wooden cupboard was painted freehand and distressed using varnish and artists' oil paints (see pp. 150–151).*

Doors and Architraves

DOORS COMPLEMENT the main area of decoration, the walls, and they are usually tackled after the walls and before the rest of the woodwork. Before starting you need to decide whether both sides of the door are to be treated in the same way, and, if not, where the decoration will stop. You should also remove the door furniture, like handles and knobs, since painting around obstacles will interrupt your flow.

A finish which is typically used on doors is dragging (see pp. 64–66), carried out in a certain order (see below). It can be done in any colour but a classic treatment uses light, grey-brown over off-white, a neutral colour combination which will work well with most wall colours.

Woodgraining (see pp. 104–111) is a popular treatment for doors, with the more expensive, richly-coloured woods, such as mahogany, bird's-eye maple, oak, or walnut being imitated.

Marbling (see pp. 74–89) only works in the context of total fantasy. Logic tells us that what is usually made of wood cannot be made from a heavy slab of cold marble.

The architrave is the moulding around the door opening which frames the door when it is closed. It can be treated in the same way as the door or the wall, or individually. The architrave serves as a break between the wall and the door and should be treated accordingly. For instance, if both the door and walls have strong decoration you might consider leaving the architrave plain.

The simplest treatment for an architrave is to apply glaze and wipe it off with a cloth, leaving colour in the mouldings. Marbled architraves are more complicated to produce, but can look very effective (see p. 161). You will need to use a stippling brush to soften the effect instead of a softening brush.

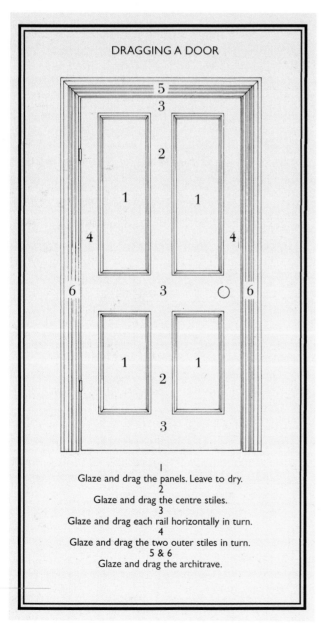

DRAGGING A DOOR

1
Glaze and drag the panels. Leave to dry.
2
Glaze and drag the centre stiles.
3
Glaze and drag each rail horizontally in turn.
4
Glaze and drag the two outer stiles in turn.
5 & 6
Glaze and drag the architrave.

LEFT AND OPPOSITE TOP *An inexpensive flush door can be made to look grand by first attaching moulding to it. To complete the effect, the door and architrave are woodgrained in bird's-eye maple, to match the dado and woodwork.*

LEFT AND OPPOSITE LEFT *Both the door and architrave have been classically treated by dragging light brown over an ivory base coat.*

LEFT AND OPPOSITE CENTRE *The panels of this hall door were ragged in mid-yellow and the mouldings were highlighted using a green glaze applied with a rag. The main frame was dragged and the architrave painted using the same yellow, which matches the wall.*

LEFT AND OPPOSITE RIGHT *Mahogany is a very expensive wood, but you can achieve the same richness and opulence with a painted finish on a cheaper door. Here the door and the architrave have been given the mahogany effect, as has the dado and woodwork.*

Dados, Radiators, and Skirtings

THE DADO IS THE AREA underneath the chair rail or dado rail, an 18th-century device introduced to protect the wall from damage from chairs. It eventually evolved into a wall divider, positioned at different heights – for instance, dados in Edwardian houses can be very high – and has lost its original function. Dado rails became unfashionable in the 1950s and 1960s, but are now popular again as their effectiveness has been rediscovered and their place seen in the period home.

A dado provides all sorts of scope for decoration, and if the rail has been removed at some point in your room's history, then replacements can be bought. You can also paint a false dado rail, either as a trompe-l'oeil effect, or as a simple line in a dark paint colour.

The dado area is usually darker than the rest of the wall, acting as an anchor to the room. Traditionally, the wall might be dragged above and marbled below (see pp. 64–66, 74–89, and 168) or stippled below trompe-l'oeil panels (see pp. 54–55

and 130–131). The rail itself can be colour wiped or dragged. Many faux finishes, such as porphyry and woodgraining (see pp. 94–95 and 104–111), are also suitable for the dado.

Anaglypta, a type of raised wallpaper made to look like old, Spanish raised leather, was sometimes pasted on the dado, especially in Edwardian houses.

Nowadays many people cover radiators, which then provides an attractive area for decoration – dragging is popular on radiator covers. Otherwise it is difficult to reach behind a radiator so the professional thing to do is to first remove it so that it can be decorated properly. Needless to say, radiators should be switched off before they are painted!

The scope for finishes on radiators depends on their shape; try ragging, sponging, and marbling (see pp. 50–51 and 58–61). Help them to disappear by blending them in with the colour and finish of the wall or woodwork. The heat from a radiator will make a conventional oil-based glaze mixture go yellow but a water-based glaze is not affected by the heat.

Skirting-boards/baseboards are often in bad condition because they tend to get knocked by furniture and kicked by people. If they are in good condition or have been replaced, a simple solution is dragging. Marbled finishes work well although are time-consuming to do. The skirting-board/baseboard and dado can be marbled to blend in with each other. Alternatively, they can be ragged in strong colours, or ragged twice in similar colours to imitate marble and then varnished with a matt, oil-based varnish (see pp. 44–45) to protect them from everyday wear and tear.

OPPOSITE *The skirting-board/baseboard, dado, and dado rail have been marbled in deep crimson over bright pink. Before starting, the dado was divided into slabs with a soft pencil. The wall above the dado was stippled with the same colour combination.*

RIGHT AND FAR RIGHT *These radiators have been successfully merged into a marble-effect background.*

ABOVE *The dado rail was dragged using a mixture of colours and, when it was partially dry and the glaze was sticky, it was wiped with a cloth. The patches of dark paint above the dado rail add to the antique effect.*

LEFT *A deep and heavy Victorian skirting-board/baseboard and architrave were painted to match a real marble fireplace elsewhere in the room. The marbling was done in several stages and then varnished to protect it from scuff marks and scratches.*

Ceilings and Cornices

THE INACCESSIBILITY OF ceilings makes painting them in special finishes quite difficult. Colourwashing is the easiest to apply (see pp. 62–63), and skies and clouds are also a possibility (see pp. 134–135). A decorative effect on the ceiling should be considered very carefully and in relation to the treatment of the walls.

Ceilings are usually painted a few tones lighter than the walls, but they should not be dramatically contrasting and off-white is preferable to stark white. Rooms in older-style houses, however, may have disproportionately high ceilings which benefit from a dark treatment. This gives the effect of lowering the ceiling height, making a more cosy, intimate atmosphere. Pale wall colours can be continued on the ceiling.

Colourwashing is the easiest technique to carry out on a ceiling. A floor mop can be wrapped in cloth and used to reach the ceiling. It is a bit unwieldy but very effective. You may be able to find the very large stippling brushes with pole attachments which are made for decorating large public areas and could use this to stipple (see pp. 54–55) a ceiling. In a small area, a ceiling can be made into a feature by printing with a sponge, which is very quick and direct. A simple pattern such as a chequered design would be very effective.

The cornice acts as a transition between the colour of the walls and the ceiling, so decorate it in a tone between the two to act as intermediary, especially where the wall is quite dark and the ceiling light. The easiest finish for a cornice is to wipe it with glaze colour; stipple it first to spread the glaze and stop it settling in any dips, before wiping with a soft cloth. A marbled cornice is very sophisticated and works well when the colours are kept light (see pp. 74–89). If you have an ornate cornice do not be tempted to pick out the shapes in different colours. It provides too much focus in the wrong area and is too fussy. If you do not have a cornice you might like to stencil (see pp. 114–119) or freehand paint a border around the top of the wall to act as the transition between wall and ceiling.

The frieze is the space between the picture rail and ceiling and is a good area for freehand painting or stencilling. Remember to keep the colours light to prevent the design seeming oppressive. The picture rail can be dragged (see pp. 64–66) or painted in with the rest of the room.

1 The best way to decorate a moulded cornice to give depth and highlights is to first apply a coat of glaze and stipple it (see p. 54) to distribute the glaze evenly.

2 Leave the glaze until it is tacky, then wipe the moulding with a cotton rag to reveal the raised pattern.

ABOVE Because this stencil has to fit into a restricted space, it is important that it retains a feeling of rhythm, rather than having a static quality. Although the design is derived quite faithfully from the curtain fabric, the stencil has been cut in a much looser and freer manner.

OPPOSITE A border, based on the motifs of the curtain fabric, was stencilled just below the cornice, giving the effect of a frieze. Although the design repeats itself in some places, it has a generally free, uninhibited feel.

LEFT To provide a transition from the grey walls to the lighter ceiling, the plastered beams and cornice were painted in a light marble, using various tones of grey.

Mantelpieces

THE FIREPLACE IS THE focal point of a room, and it is a good idea to treat it differently from the surrounding walls. If the fireplace is actually used for fires then paint is perfectly safe as long as there are slips separating the fire from the mantelpiece. Mutton clothing and stippling are the simplest classic techniques (see pp. 48–49 and 54–55), especially on raised or carved areas which can be wiped gently with a soft cloth to reveal the base colour. Ragging and colourwashing (see pp. 50–51 and 62–63) are particularly effective on a plain mantelpiece.

Marbling is a popular technique (see pp. 74–89); the whole mantelpiece is treated as one large piece of marble, rather than lots of blocks. Use a stippling brush to soften marbling on a carved mantelpiece since softening brushes only wipe the glaze off the raised areas, instead of blending it. Other faux finishes such as woodgraining (see pp. 104–111), and inlays in malachite or porphyry (see pp. 90–95) also work well.

Freehand painting, stencilling, stamping, or ageing with wax or varnish (see pp. 114–125 and 150–153) will enhance any mantelpiece.

ABOVE *This cast-iron mantelpiece has been marbled in shades of sand and brown. The generous veining gives the impression that the mantelpiece has been carved from a single block of marble.*

OPPPOSITE *This mantelpiece has been stippled with a mix of light grey and raw umber to match the marbled dado. The mouldings were wiped with a cloth to reveal the base colour.*

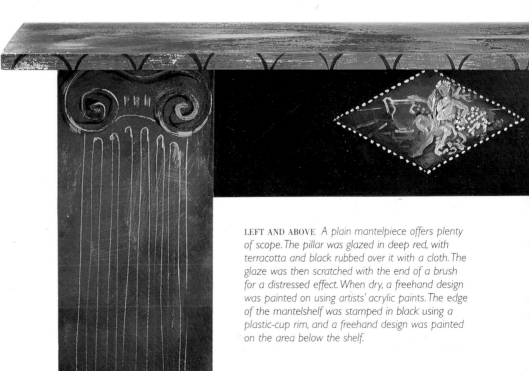

LEFT AND ABOVE *A plain mantelpiece offers plenty of scope. The pillar was glazed in deep red, with terracotta and black rubbed over it with a cloth. The glaze was then scratched with the end of a brush for a distressed effect. When dry, a freehand design was painted on using artists' acrylic paints. The edge of the mantelshelf was stamped in black using a plastic-cup rim, and a freehand design was painted on the area below the shelf.*

Windows and Shutters

OST WINDOW DECORATION is provided by curtains, but there is scope for using decorative paint finishes on shutters, around the window frame, on pelmets, and even on the window panes themselves.

Shutters are like doors and so provide a good area for dragging, woodgraining, freehand painting, or stencilling (see pp. 64–66, 104–111, and 114–119). If there are no curtains the window can be framed with a border of stencilling or freehand painting. The bars of windows are really too small to paint decoratively, so simply paint them in a light colour which will not contrast with the bright outside.

Spray paints can be used to stencil simple designs on glass window panes, although washing the windows afterwards has to be done with great care.

ABOVE *The shutters and wainscot have been dragged in a mix of burnt umber and white to complement pink, ragged walls (see pp. 50–51). The window frames have been simply wiped with a cloth dipped in glaze.*

RIGHT *A small, square, cloakroom window has been spray-painted in several colours on overlapping stencils, thus providing privacy. Fern motifs were chosen to merge with the garden outside.*

ABOVE *Curtains are not needed on this window, so a border has been painted around it for interest. A little water-based paint was applied around a leaf shape cut from cardboard.*

OPPOSITE *The mouldings and shutters were used as picture frames to create these charming, stylized paintings in a children's room.*

Halls, Banisters, and Stairs

CORRIDORS, LANDINGS, and halls should be welcoming, interesting, and friendly. They give first impressions to guests and link the different parts of the house. The hall should therefore bring together the different elements and atmospheres of the surrounding rooms.

A simple hall and landing solution would be to keep these areas neutral, which can mean they end up looking bland and uninteresting. This does not have to be the case however. Because these areas are only seen in passing, colours can be bright and the finishes strong and interesting. For instance, a dense stencilled effect, stripes, inlaid designs of malachite on black along a dado, or a strong colourwash (see pp. 114–119, 126, 90–93, and 62–63) all look great in the hall and also provide a good backdrop for a collection of framed pictures. Take care, however, if the hall is narrow since visual excitement can crowd it, making it look like a tunnel. In this case choose a soft colour for any pattern making. If the hall is dark, use a bright colour like yellow to reflect the light and bring a bit of life into it. The same colour on the ceiling should open it up a bit more too.

It is difficult to work around banisters so do not take on anything which is going to be too time-consuming. Quick and plain techniques that work well are mutton clothing and ragging (see pp. 48–51), or simply wiping over the banister with a rag dipped in glaze.

The beauty of staircases is that they are viewed from all sorts of angles, with continuous changes of viewpoint as you ascend and descend. This means that any part of the wall, floor, or ceiling can be decorated because it will be viewed at some point. The problem with decorating the walls and ceiling is reaching them. You must use some form of scaffolding, usually a system of planking, step ladders, and support from a friend, and very long brushes! Like hallways and corridors the staircase can end up rather bland, whereas the staircase walls actually provide a wonderful opportunity for using interesting or strong effects in bright colours.

Skirting-boards/baseboards are important on staircases because they are much more conspicuous here than in any other area of the home, and they should be decorated to provide a link between the carpet and the wall. Dragging (see pp. 64–66) is probably the easiest technique, but marbling and oak, bird's-eye maple, or walnut woodgraining (see pp. 74–89 and 104–109) can also work very well.

The stairs themselves can be decorated, perhaps like a simplified carpet pattern using stencils or a freehand, repeating motif. Some older houses still have a stair rail, if yours has not, you can either fit a new rail, or paint a false dado rail where the stair rail used to be. This could be a trompe-l'oeil effect, or, more simply, a masked-out line or freehand brush line (see p. 127).

ABOVE *Banisters are fiddly to work with, and so need to be painted in a way that is not too time-consuming. These banisters were ragged in mid-yellow over off-white, and then ragged again in mid-green.*

LEFT *This hall has been given a traditional look by painting the dado in marble panels.*

ABOVE A trompe-l'oeil rope and garland makes an attractive feature of this spiral staircase. Chevrons have been stencilled on the stair treads.

LEFT In this classical approach, the newel posts have been dragged and the banisters mutton clothed.

RIGHT A more elaborate and time-consuming approach is to paint a marble effect on each banister. The results are magnificent, if you have the patience.

Floors

NOW THAT PAINT and a feeling for the decorative have been rediscovered, a mass of new, old, and seductive ideas for decorating floors has opened up, and a painted floor presents a more individual, conscious sense of style than the usual carpet or tiles.

The beauty of paint lies in its flexibility and potential visual impact: in the formal or informal use of pattern, in washed-out finishes, in crisply-delineated designs, in classic symmetry and sophisticated colour – the possibilities are limitless. The other advantage is cost; paint is a cheap form of floor covering and can, therefore, be changed with comparative ease when the room is redecorated.

Designs can be applied directly on to bare wooden boards, painted boards, or concrete or hardboard floors. Floors can be marbled (see pp. 74–89), inlaid with malachite, porphyry, or granite (see pp. 90–95 and 99), hand painted with a trompe-l'oeil rug design or decorated with stencils (see pp. 114–119), placed randomly or following a grid.

Painted floors are much more practical than most people imagine. There is no need to use special floor paint, and paint adheres very well to wooden floors. All painted floors should be given a few coats of varnish (see pp. 44–45), concrete floors especially so. When protected in this way the decoration wears extremely well and the floor is easily cleaned.

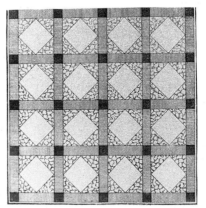

ABOVE, LEFT, AND OPPOSITE *These floor designs are taken from John Carwitham's* Various Kinds of Floor Decoration *(1739). Originally they were designed as patterns for stone or marble floors, or painted floorcloths. They are suitable for translating on to a floor using a variety of finishes and colours.*

The designs can be painted over a base coat using water-based paints. Taking one colour at a time, the different areas can be masked off with tape (see p. 126), or drawn freehand.

LEFT *A trompe-l'oeil rug has been painted on this cloakroom floor. This is a relatively quick and inexpensive way to add a stylish touch of humour to an otherwise plain floor. The concrete floor was given several coats of base colour and the rug was painted using artists' acrylic paints and then varnished. An area like this that will have heavy wear requires a minimum of seven coats of durable varnish.*

BELOW *A wooden floor in bad condition can be covered quite cheaply and to good effect with hardboard squares. Those shown were first painted in a loose, haphazard manner before being stencilled.*

ABOVE *A border of leaves in a flowing design was stencilled on the wood-block floor of this hall. It follows the curve of the wall and flows around the shape of the newel post, making an unusual and eye-catching feature.*

RIGHT *A large area can be covered fairly quickly with floating marble (see pp. 84–85). After this entire floor was marbled, it was divided into squares and alternate squares were painted with a thin mixture of blue glaze, allowing the underlying pattern of the marble to show through.*

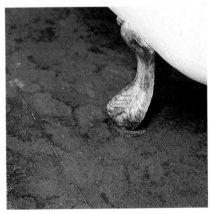

TOP *This floor was colourwashed (see pp. 62–63) over a geometric pattern made of masking tape; successive layers of tape were peeled off at various stages.*

ABOVE *Indigo-coloured floating marble (see pp. 84–85) was applied over a bright blue base coat, with deep red added in small patches. The floor was well varnished to withstand the rigours of constant splashing.*

RIGHT *Plain and practical coir matting has been given a traditional border design. The design was painted freehand with artists' acrylic paint.*

Furniture

THERE IS A WIDE and varied pool of potential sources of inspiration for painting furniture, from ancient to modern. The folk art of provincial America with its wide mix of European influences, the sophisticated French and Italian styles, and Scandinavian elegance are amongst the best known. In the 20th century, probably the most famous bright and creative style was produced by the Bloomsbury artists under Duncan Grant and Vanessa Bell. Each style and time has produced its own colours and motifs, each country its own particular character. Whether you single out individual aspects or set out to copy meticulously, you can be certain of producing your own unique pieces of furniture.

There are two positions to start from when decorating furniture. The first is to take inspiration from your needs and let them dictate the style of decoration. For example, if you need a small bedside cupboard for a guest bedroom, you should choose colours and a style which complement the other decorations in the room. Alternatively you can start with a technique that really interests you. In this case you will need to work on a plain item such as a tray or frame so that the technique can be explored as fully as possible.

Before you embark on your decoration, consider the style of your chosen piece. An art-deco-style cupboard cannot be transformed into a Victorian-style bijou piece without radical surgery. Similarly, a fine piece with pretty, delicate tracery will not marry well with a robust, country style of painting.

Whatever you decide, try not to use too many techniques and colours on a single item, as the effect is likely to become gaudy and overpowering. Three or four tones with a similar number of colours should be your limit.

LEFT *The back and rim of the seat of this 19th-century chair have been painted in a malachite inlay (see pp. 90–93) with a black outline for contrast. On the front of the legs, two little medallions of malachite with a gold border provide a focus.*

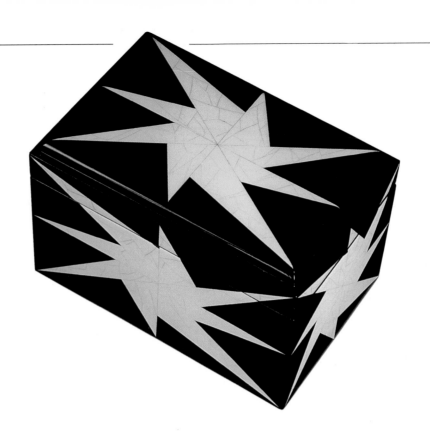

RIGHT *This decorated box has a contemporary feel even though the star shapes have been crackle varnished (see pp. 146–147), a technique usually administered as an ageing effect. The sharp edges, unusual star design, and the glossy, varnished black all contribute to the contemporary look. Painted by Peter Davey.*

ABOVE *The dark case of this old piano was beyond repair and so was given a new lease of life by stencilling (see pp. 114–119) with elegant but vigorous garlands of flowers and fruit. It was then aged with coloured varnishes (see pp. 150–151). Painted by Liz Macfarlane.*

RIGHT *This chest of drawers was inspired by an 18th-century Venetian piece of furniture. The white paint was given an aged patina by applying two coloured waxes in dark shades, which were toned down by buffing with a soft cloth (see p. 45). The edges were gilded using metallic wax (see pp. 144–145).*

BELOW *This frame was painted in artists' acrylic paints in umbers, ochres, and siennas over a buff-coloured glaze (see pp. 100–101). The tortoiseshell effect was finished with several coats of high-gloss varnish (see p. 44).*

BELOW *Decorated tin is also known as tôle ware. This cachepot was painted red then decorated with bronze powders (see pp. 144–145). Decorated by Golfar and Hughes.*

RIGHT *Over a mottle, sea-green background, paper cut-out fish and other sea creatures swim around this paper-chained trunk. The crackle-varnished finish (see pp. 146–147) gives both depth and age to the effect. Decorated by Nicola Wingate-Saul.*

ABOVE *The shape of this pretty table is softened and enhanced by stencilling (see pp. 114–119) using olive-green, blues, and terracotta in a fleur-de-lis and leaf design over pale blue-grey. The paint was rubbed back with wax and steel wool to give a worn look (see pp. 152–153).*

RIGHT *A wooden column has been marbled in a delightfully dramatic and expressive way and spattered with artists' oil paints thinned with turpentine (see pp. 74–79 and 96–97). The darker painted base gives the piece a feeling of solidity. Painted by Pamela Griffiths.*

ABOVE *This china lamp base was covered with crackleglaze and then painted all over in deep, earthy red (see pp. 148–149). The design on top was painted freehand, using a 17th-century Dutch painting as inspiration.*

RIGHT *The square shape of copper leaf was put to use on this cupboard to make a grid pattern (see pp. 138–139). The leaf was aged with coarse steel wool to reveal some of the dark green base.*

BELOW *A panel in the centre of this green table has been painted with a Vert Antique marble which looks inlaid (see pp. 74–83 and 88–89). The cream lining (see p. 127) and painting on the legs helps to bring the whole piece together. Painted by Lady Daphne.*

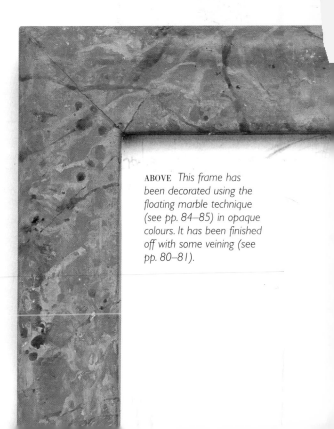

ABOVE *This frame has been decorated using the floating marble technique (see pp. 84–85) in opaque colours. It has been finished off with some veining (see pp. 80–81).*

ABOVE *The outline of the gold convolvulus was applied using a stencil and transfer Dutch metal leaf (see pp. 114–119 and 138–139). After varnishing, the details were hand painted in over the gold. By Michael Midgely.*

BELOW *Plinths for small statues or objets d'art were often made from decorative stones like marble or porphyry. These two have been painted to imitate malachite (left) and lapis lazuli (right) (see pp. 90–93 and 96–97). Painted by Felicity Wakefield.*

ABOVE *The dark base of this little bedside cupboard was lightly painted in a lighter top-coat colour. In the panels, shapes reminiscent of a grille were stencilled before the whole piece was distressed with wax (see pp. 114–119 and 152–153).*

ABOVE *The decoration for the cupboard panels was inspired by a Japanese kimono fabric. A tartan effect was made by combing in blue and red over a yellow base (see pp. 68–69). A random arrangement of blue foliage was stencilled all over the panels and the framework of the doors was given a casual chequered effect by using the edge of some firm thick cardboard to stamp in yellow (see pp. 114–119 and 124).*

LEFT *This Swedish tilt-top table (circa 1880) displays a traditional but idiosyncratic style of painted decoration. The same type of look could be achieved by using a blue glaze and swirling it like a decorative walnut grain (see pp. 108–109). The base can be achieved by distressing a blue-grey paint with wax (see pp. 152–153).*

RIGHT *A 19th-century tea canister was restored using transfer Dutch metal leaf over black paint (see pp. 138–139). The leaf has been protected with oil-based varnish (see pp. 44–45).*

LEFT A simple, flat frame provides a great base for showing off paint finishes. From left to right these frames have been sponged on in deep red over red, crackle varnished over creamy-brown, woodgrained in ochre bird's-eye maple over pale yellow, combed in dark blue over bright mid-blue, and given a malachite finish with transfer Dutch metal leaf edging (see pp. 58–59, 146–147, 106–107, 68–69, 90–93, and 138–139).

BELOW Inspired by a 4,000-year-old piece of Egyptian pottery this string box was painted in mid-blue over a deep red background then hand painted with the figure of a lion. The whole box was varnished and scratched and the scratches accentuated with paint (see pp. 150–151).

ABOVE The warm, aged look of this pretty 19th-century French table can be achieved with either a warm-coloured wax or a yellowed varnish (see pp. 44–45). The decoration would probably originally have been hand painted in the traditional style but it could be recreated using stencils (see pp. 114–119) supplemented with a little freehand painting.

Glossary

A

Acetate Transparent or semi-transparent film used for making stencils.

Acrylic size See *gold size*

Acrylic varnish See *varnish*

Ageing Techniques that simulate the effect of time and wear on a freshly-painted surface. Also called *antiquing*.

Aluminium leaf A less expensive alternative to *silver leaf*, used for *gilding*.

Antiquing Techniques that simulate the effect of time and wear on a freshly-painted surface. Also called *ageing*.

Architrave The wooden frame surrounding a door or window. It can be simple, moulded, and ornate.

Artists' acrylic paints Fast-drying water-based paint that dries to a waterproof finish. Used by decorators for tinting water-based *glaze*.

Artists' oil paints Oil paints used by decorators for tinting oil-based *glaze*. They can also be thinned with *turpentine* for freehand painting.

B

Badger-hair softening brush See *softening brush*

Base coat The first coat of paint, applied before the *glaze* coat. The base coat is painted in a non-absorbent paint such as a mid-sheen, water-based paint like *vinyl silk/satin latex* when working with water-based glazes or a mid-sheen, oil-based paint such as oil *eggshell* as the base for oil-based glazes.

Bole A coloured clay mixed with *rabbit-skin glue* and used to colour *gesso* before *traditional gilding*.

Border A design around the edge of a panel, wall, floor, etc. It can be *stencilled*, *stamped*, or painted freehand.

Brass leaf See *Dutch metal leaf*

Bridge Small tabs left in place in a cut-out *stencil* to prevent it 'falling out'.

Bronze powders Metallic powders available in several shades and used with *gold size* or *wax* to create *gilded* effects.

Burnisher Extremely smooth agate polisher used for burnishing gold to a high shine in *traditional gilding*.

C

Chair rail See *dado rail*

Comb Rubber or cardboard toothed implements, originally developed for woodgraining techniques and now also used for combing. Can be commercial or home-made.

Copper leaf A *metal leaf* used in *gilding*.

Cornice Moulding around a room between the walls and ceiling, traditionally found built in position, but nowadays prefabricated.

Craft knife A very sharp knife with replaceable blades, used to cut *stencils* from stencil card.

Crackleglaze An *antiquing* medium used between two layers of paint. The top paint layer reacts with the crackleglaze and forms cracks, revealing the base colour.

Crackle varnish An *antiquing* technique using two varnishes that work against each other to produce a crazed effect.

D

Dado The part of the wall beneath the *dado rail*, traditionally painted, panelled, or otherwise decorated differently from the rest of the wall.

Dado rail A rail, developed in the 18th century, fixed to walls to prevent damage from chair backs. Also known as chair rails.

Distressing Any technique that simulates the effects of wear and tear on a newly-painted surface. Also used to describe the technique for breaking up the *glaze* coat in marbling.

Dragging brush A coarse, long-bristled brush originally used for woodgraining and now also used for dragging.

Driers Chemicals mixed with paint and *glaze* to accelerate the drying process.

Dutch metal leaf A less expensive, and easier to use, alternative to real *gold leaf*, used for *gilding*.

E

Eggshell A mid-sheen paint used as a *base coat* for basic and faux finishes.

Emulsion/latex See *matt emulsion/flat latex*

F

Fitch Hog-hair brush used in many techniques and as an alternative to the household paintbrush. The five types are round, filbert, long, short, and herkomer.

Flogging brush Coarse horse-hair, long-bristled brush originally used for woodgraining techniques and now also used for flogging.

Floor paint A range of very tough paint suitable for use on wood, linoleum, or concrete.

Frieze The area of a wall between the *cornice* and *picture rail*. Also a band of decoration, usually just below the cornice, that may be wallpapered, *stencilled*, or painted freehand.

Fuso A machine used for spraying paint, rather like coarse spattering.

G

Gesso A white substance prepared with *rabbit-skin glue* and *whiting* and applied to surfaces in many layers to give a completely smooth finish. Essential in *traditional gilding*.

Gilder's knife A well-balanced knife used for cutting *gold leaf*.

Gilder's pad A pad with a soft folding wall of parchment used to hold and protect the delicate *gold leaf* in *traditional gilding*.

Gilder's tip A specialist tool made of hairs sandwiched between two pieces of very thin cardboard, used to pick up *gold leaf* in *traditional gilding*.

Gilding The technique of giving a surface a metallic finish using real *gold leaf*, *imitation metal leaf* or *bronze powders*. See also *traditional gilding*.

Glaze A colourless, slow-drying, transparent medium to which colour is added in the form of paint or pigment. Used for most paint effects. Traditionally, oil-based glazes were used and mixed with varying degrees of *white spirit/mineral spirits* and *artists' oil paints*. Oil-based glazes are being replaced by good-quality water-based glazes which are odourless and easier to use. Oil-based glazes are still used for some faux finish techniques. Precoloured glazes are also available.

Gold leaf Sheets of gold beaten to wafer thinness and used in *traditional gilding*.

Gold size A special glue used to adhere *metal leaf* and *bronze powders*. Available as a water-based system sometimes called acrylic size and as an oil-based product.

H

Heartgrainer A specialist tool used to imitate the heart grain of oak and pine. Also used to give the effect of moire silk.

Hog-hair softening brush See *softening brush*

I

Imitation metal leaf The less-expensive, and easier to use, alternative to real *gold* and *silver* leaf. Used for gilding. See also *Dutch metal leaf* and *aluminium leaf*.

L

Lining A technique for outlining the shape of a surface with one or more decorative lines.

Lining brush See *swordliner*

Lining paper Plain, flat wallpaper used to line the walls of a room, often to disguise the poor quality of the plaster.

Linseed oil A yellow vegetable oil; one of the main ingredients of oil-based *glaze*.

Loose metal Metal leaf used for gilding. The sheets must be handled with care. Available in all the metals – *copper, Dutch metal, gold, silver,* and *aluminium*.

Low-vinyl paint A specialist decorator's paint which has a low plastic content. It is ideal for all paint techniques including colouring water-based *glaze*, *stencilling*, freehand painting, and *antiquing* techniques. Available from specialist paint shops.

M

Masking tape A self-adhesive tape with many uses, including masking areas you do not want decorated and acting as guide lines for painting straight lines.

Matt emulsion/ flat latex A flat, water-based paint used to colour *glaze*.

Megilp An old-fashioned name for *glaze*.

Metal leaf Sheets of very thin, beaten metal available in *loose* and *transfer* forms and used for *gilding*. See also *aluminium leaf, copper leaf, Dutch metal leaf, gold leaf, imitation metal leaf,* and *silver leaf*.

Methylated spirits An alcohol-based solvent used for cleaning brushes and in some marble techniques.

Mineral spirits See *white spirit/mineral spirits*

Mottler A specialist brush used for wood-graining techniques. The three main types are long-haired, short-haired, and wavy.

Moulding Ornamental plasterwork or woodwork outlines.

Mutton cloth Also known as stockinet, this cotton cloth with a variable weave is used for mutton clothing and lifting off surplus *glaze* in many faux finish techniques.

O

Oil-based glaze See *glaze*

Oil size See *gold size*

Overgrainer A specialist brush used for *overgraining*.

Overgraining Painting a second layer of graining lines in woodgraining techniques.

P

Paint kettle A small, bucket-like container, made of plastic or metal, in which small quantities of paint can be carried easily.

Palette Tray used for mixing paint. Also the term used to describe the range of colours used by an artist or decorator.

Patina A surface film produced by age.

Patinating medium A water-based medium which gives a surface the effect of *patina*.

Patination The method of imitating a *patina*. Usually involves *wax* or *patinating medium*.

Peeling paint medium See *crackleglaze*

Picture rail Horizontal *moulding* originally designed for hanging pictures. Usually about 43cm (17in) from the *cornice*.

Pigment Colouring matter used in paint. Powder pigments are available from specialist art shops and can be used to colour your own *glaze, varnish,* or *wax*.

Polyurethane varnish See *varnish*

Primary colours The colours from which all other colours can be mixed – red, yellow, and blue. They combine to form *secondary colours*.

Primer A sealant used on new plaster or woodwork before painting.

R

Rabbit-skin glue Glue made of animal skin used in making *gesso and bole* and making the size for *traditional gilding*. Available in sheet and granule forms.

Rail The horizontal sections in the main frame of a panelled door.

Registration marks Guides used to indicate the position of subsequent *stencils* if you are *stencilling* a repeat design or using more than one stencil.

Rigger Artist's brush with long hairs.

S

Sable brush Artist's high-quality brush.

Sandpaper Abrasive paper available in varying degrees of coarseness. Used to make a surface smooth.

Scumble Another name for *glaze*.

Secondary colours Colours made by mixing two *primary colours*. When mixed together they form *tertiary colours*.

Shellac See *varnish*

Silver leaf Sheets of silver beaten to wafer thinness and used in *gilding*.

Size See *gold size*

Softening brush A long-haired brush used for softening and blending coloured *glaze*, especially in faux finish techniques. Badger-hair softening brushes are easier to use than hog-hair softening brushes, but are more expensive.

Spirit level   A glass tube partly filled with spirit; the position of the air bubble indicates horizontality.

Stainers   Sometimes known as universal stainers and used to colour *glaze*.

Stamping   Paint is applied over a three-dimensional motif carved from blocks of wood, polystyrene, sponges, or fruit and vegetables, and pressed against the surface, leaving a print of the motif.

Steel wool   An abrasive made from fine shavings of steel; available in varying degrees of coarseness.

Stencil   The cut-out design used for *stencilling*. Can be cut from *acetate* or specialist stencil card. Ready-cut and ready-printed stencils are also available.

Stencil brush   Short-haired brush designed to hold a small amount of paint. Available in a wide range of sizes and with long or short handles.

Stencilling   A decorative technique in which paint is applied through a cut-out motif.

Stile   The vertical sections in the main frame of a panelled door.

Stippling brush   A specialist brush used for the stippling technique and for removing excess paint from *cornices* and *architraves*, etc. Available in a variety of sizes.

Stockinet   See *mutton cloth*

Straight-edge   A metal edge used for drawing and cutting straight lines.

Swordliner   Specialist paintbrush that tapers to a point. Used for *lining* and *veining* marbles. Available in sizes 0 to 3.

T

Tertiary colours   Colours made by mixing two *secondary colours.*

Tone   The term used to describe how dark or light a colour is. Different colours can be the same tone.

Traditional gilding   The specialized technique for applying real *gold leaf* to a surface.

Transfer metal leaf   Used for *gilding*, a more expensive but easier to use alternative to *loose metal leaf*. The metal leaf comes with a waxed-paper backing that makes it easier to handle.

Trompe-l'oeil   A two-dimensional painting designed to deceive the viewers into believing that they are seeing a three-dimensional scene or object.

Turpentine   A resinous solvent mixed in some paints and *varnishes*. Use to thin *artists' oil paints*.

U

Undercoat   Matt paint applied to a surface before the *base coat*.

V

Varnish   A transparent protective coat applied to completed paint finishes. Varnishes may be matt, mid-sheen/satin, or gloss. They are available as a water-based product, also known as acrylic varnish, and oil-based, also known as polyurethane varnish. Spirit-based varnishes are known as shellac.

Varnish brush   A specialist, flat-ended brush with quite long bristles, used to apply *varnish*.

Veining   The technique of painting veins on simulated marble.

Vinyl silk/ satin latex   A water-based paint with a mid-sheen, used as a *base coat*.

W

Water-based glaze   See *glaze*

Wax   A protective medium which works by penetrating an absorbent surface. Wax can be clear or dark: dark wax colours the surface.

Wet-and-dry sandpaper   Abrasive used with water to achieve a very smooth surface.

Whiting   Finely-ground calcium carbonate used in making *gesso*.

White spirit/ mineral spirits   Mineral solvent mixed in varying proportions with oil-based *glaze* and *artists' oil paints*.

Index

Acknowledgements

We are grateful to all the decorative painters who contributed to the book,
especially the late Victoria Morland whose beautiful box so graciously punctuates the title pages.

The authors and publisher would like to thank the following artists and decorators for
kindly allowing their work to be photographed.

Felicity Binyon and Elizabeth Macfarlane Stencil Designs 118, 119T, 119C, 162T, 163T, 172TR,
172BL, 174–175B; James Booth 168L; Chalon 182L; Serena Chaplin 140–141; Lady Daphne 179BL;
Peter Davey 175T, 176BL; Victoria Ellerton 90, 126BL; David Genty 48, 49BL, 55BL, 164; Golfar and
Hughes 100R, 176BR, 182B; Elaine Green 114–115, 119B, 156, 166B; Pamela Griffiths 165T, 169R,
178R; Belinda Hextall 143L; Sally Kenny 97R; François Lavenir 145BL; Harry Levinson 105B, 106L,
110R, 159T, 159BR; Michael Midgley 180T; Victoria Moreland 1, 3, 89B, 106R (for Colefax & Fowler);
Caroline Richardson 159BL; Valerie Traynor 133B, 135C; Felicity Wakefield 94R, 161BL, 180B, 135B;
Nicola Wingate-Saul 177T.

The authors and publisher would like to thank the following people for their
help with step-by-step photography.

Felicity Binyon (stencilling), Dorothy Boyer (trompe-l'oeil), and Belinda Hextall (traditional gilding),
François Lavenir (bronze powders), Valerie Traynor (stone blocks and skies).

The authors and publisher would like to thank the following people for kindly allowing
their houses, etc. to be photographed.

Beaudesert 10–11, 55T, 57, 66T, 75T, 86, 100L, 108, 110L, 159BL, 160, 161T, 162T, 163, 166TL,
168L, 169BL, 180B; Carola Bird 126BL; Chatsworth House 128L; Colour Counsellors 119T; Carrie
Hinton 165T; Mrs Hume-Kendall 48, 49BL, 55BL; Helena Mercer 159BC, 168R, 174L, 183BR;
National Trust 7; 130L; Mrs Sasse 164; Hamish Scott-Dalgleish 90; Louise Wigley 9.

The authors and publisher would like to thank the following sources for their kind permission
to reproduce the photographs listed.

Jon Bouchier 9, 49T and colourways, 50, 51T, C, and colourways, 52, 53TL, 54, 55T and colourways,
57T, C, and colourways, 58, 59T, C, and colourways, 60, 61T and colourways, 63T, C, and colourways,
64, 65T, BL, and colourways, 66BL and BR, 67, 68–70, 71T, C, and colourways, 75T, 76–88, 90–92,
93T, C, and BL, 94R. 95, 96, 97TL, CL, BL, and colourways, 99, 101, 102–111, 116–117, 118T,
119BR, 120–121, 122TL, 123, 124, 126T and BR, 127L, 128R, 129, 131, 135B, 139C and B,
142–143, 156, 157TL, 159T and BR, 160, 161T and BL, 162–163, 168L, 169TL, 172TL, 173T and
BL; Geoff Dann 26–39, 42–45, 53B and colourways, 56B, 61BL, 62B, 65BC, 71BL, 132–133, 134,
135T and C, 138–141, 144–153, 176T, 177, 178L, 179T, 181; Michael Dunning 12–13, 14–15, 16–17,
18–19, 20–21, 22–23, 55BC, 89TL, BR, and TR, 93R and colourways, 94L, 97R, 100, 114–115,
119CR, 121B, 125B, 127T, 157B, 165B, 169R, 172TR, 173BR, 175T, 176B, 178R, 179B, 180B,
182R, 183T; Andreas Einsiedel 2, 25C, 130BR, 161BR; Anthony Spinks 182L; Shona Wood 48L,
49B, 51B, 55BL, 59B, 63B, 66T, 157TR, 158CR, 159BL and BC, 164, 165T, 166–167, 168R,
169B, 170–171, 174L, 183BR.

You can visit Annie Sloan's internet site on www.anniesloan.com